ANARCHY IN THE SOUTH OF CONGO

Post-Civil War Rebellion

by Lazare Kokolo

Paperback ISBN: 978-0-9967310-5-8
Typesetting by Book Polishers

In loving memory of my parents

TABLE OF CONTENTS

Acknowledgements
Preface
Chapter 1: Baccalaureate Exam in Focus
Chapter 2: Kizinga
Chapter 3: The Verdict
Chapter 4: Planning for University
Chapter 5: On My Way to Mouyondzi
Chapter 6: The Inception of the Rebellion
Chapter 7: Conquering Mouyondzi
Chapter 8: Bouansa and the Aftermath
Chapter 9: United for the Cause
Chapter 10: Christmas and New Year
Chapter 11: The Nouveau Riche, Bonza Bore
Chapter 12: En Route to Nkenge
Chapter 13: At My Mother's
Chapter 14: Sadness and Joy
Chapter 15: The Race for Survival
Chapter 16: The Rest of the Family
Chapter 17: A Glimmer of Hope
Chapter 18: Braving Danger
Chapter 19: Strategizing and Planning
Chapter 20: A Trip to Mouzanga
Chapter 21: In Hindsight
Chapter 22: Flirting with Danger
Chapter 23: On the Move Again
Chapter 24: Kimfinkou
Chapter 25: Nkila-Poste Treaty
Chapter 26: The Way Forward
Chapter 27: En Route to Pointe-Noire
Chapter 28: Home Safe and Sound
Chapter 29: Asylum Overseas
Chapter 30: Lessons Learned and Reflections

ACKNOWLEDGEMENTS

Eight years ago I finished writing my story. I set it aside and lost interest altogether. If not for my mother-in-law Roslyn Taylor and my spouse Miriam Caldwell-Kokolo encouraging me to take it a step further, I wouldn't have been motivated to follow through. So I'm thankful and grateful to both of you for encouraging me to make this project happen.

Trying to get my story published has been a long, frustrating, and intense learning process. I wanted to give up. I had to delve into repressed memories and remember the horrors over the years I struggled to forget. Sections about my late father, mother, and Papa Ndazet made me experience once again the sadness of losing them and the joy they brought into my life.

So from the bottom of my heart, I would like to thank the editors, my mother-in-law Roslyn Taylor and my wife Miriam for helping me improve my manuscript. I appreciate your contributions.

Words cannot express my gratitude to the photographer, formatter, and designer for making my piece of writing visually attractive.

There wouldn't even be a book today without the people who helped me survive the rebellion, the government forces' invasion of Mouyondzi, and those who along the way facilitated my safe return to Pointe-Noire. You know who you are. I'm thankful and grateful to each one of you.

PREFACE

For a long time I struggled to tell my story. I tried to sit down and narrate it on numerous occasions. I was not strong enough to revisit that gloomy chapter of my life. The experiences I went through during the rebellion in the south of Congo were chaotic, traumatic and catastrophic. Waking up every day to the thundering sounds of machine guns, living in a state of anarchy imposed by the rebels, and later being hunted down in the forests like wild animals by government forces are not fond memories for anybody.

But, as the years passed, I grew stronger. I realized that it would be both therapeutic and imperative to share my story. Somewhere in the world, there are people enduring similar trials and tribulations or even worse. So the narrative is both their voice and cry to the world for salvation. As you read this book, I hope you hear the silent cries of those with no voices suffering in war-torn countries, and I hope it inspires you to help make this world a better place.

BACCALAUREATE EXAM IN FOCUS

As a kid growing up in the dusty streets of Pointe-Noire, my heart broke every time the innocent suffered injustice. I swore to myself that someday I had to go to law school and become an outstanding judge. Thus, to serve and help mend the chronic flaws corrupting my country's justice department became the dream. I planned on being a catalyst for positive changes. So I invested time and energy into studying hard. I knew education was the only path leading to the career of my dream. I abstained from any form of distraction. Despite the turbulent political climate, I remained optimistic for the future. Plus, I kept my sights fixed on the main aim and devised a three-step plan. The first one left me with no other option but to move out. The second was to organize a study group with my fellow students. The third and last step consisted in finding a prayer group. I couldn't afford to be sloppy. The moment came to set everything in motion. In the morning, we were sitting at the table in the kitchen playing around. I waited for my siblings to leave the room to engage our father in serious conversation.

"Dad, I want to move out," I said.

"What? You want to move out? Why now?"

"I've been s-struggling t-to con-concentrate," I stuttered.

He looked at me inquiringly, scratched his ear, and said, "Is that the solution?"

"Yes, Dad. I need to be in a much quieter environment where I can focus and concentrate."

"Oh… this is unlike you, son. What has gotten into you?"

"Dad, Voungou is full of taverns. Everybody blasts loud music from dusk till dawn, which is getting very distracting!" I replied in a frustrated tone of voice.

"Huh? Son, I've never heard you complain about this before. What's changed this time?"

"I don't want to fail my baccalaureate exam, Dad. I'm determined to do whatever it takes to pass this exam."

"Ah! Now I see. You sound like you have everything figured out. Do you have any money?"

"No, Dad. That's why I wanted to talk to you about my plan."

My father looked me in the eye with a serious look on his face, his tone of voice curious but affectionate as always, and asked, "Ah! What do you have in mind?"

I had his undivided attention and had to convince him to agree with my plan. I was nervous, which was clear in my shaky voice. I mustered up the courage to explain my reason for wanting to move.

"I spoke with Noko Loussoukou and asked him if I could stay there. Just while I'm preparing for my baccalaureate exam."

"Huh? Loussoukou? That was unwise and irresponsible. I thought I raised you better than that, son."

"I'm sorry, Dad. I'm desperate, worried, and stressed about the exam…"

"Listen, son, I'm not trying to stand in your way. I know how much making it to university means to you. And I admire your determination, focus, and efforts. However, I'm still disappointed that you didn't come to me first with your plan, before discussing it with your uncle."

"I'm sorry, Dad. Please forgive me! Don't be angry with me, please!"

"I'm not angry with you, son. Don't you ever forget that ever since your mother and I got divorced, I've been raising you guys all by myself. Not even once did any of your uncles offer to help."

"I know, Dad, and there is no confusion about that."

"I don't like asking people for favors, let alone owing Loussoukou one."

"Dad, this is temporary. I'll be staying in OCH just for six months."

"Next time you decide to make a similar plan, talk to me first, okay?"

"Yes, Dad," I said.

"You're my responsibility. Your uncles didn't get involved when you were little kids and I don't want them to get involved now."

My father fell silent, put his hand on his cheek, crossed his ankles, looked through me for a second, and turned his gaze to the window overlooking our front yard. I knew the conversation was over and I also knew where he stood on the matter. But I still sensed that a move would increase my chances of success. Besides, I believed my plan was infallible.

KIZINGA

The day before, I was at home, sitting on the front porch by the side of our street people watching, when Ntsayi dropped by.

"I'm on my way to a Kizinga in Loussala. Do you want to come along?" Ntsayi asked.

"Yes, I can't decline an invitation to a house of prayer. How far is it from here?"

"It's a 15-minute walk from here. Straight up there," he pointed with his finger, "across Terre Jaune."

"Let's get going then," I said.

We walked through our sandy street in the sweltering heat.

"I'm planning a trip to France soon, God willing. Tell nobody else. You know how people are."

"Oh! That's wonderful news, Ntsayi! Don't worry, I'm a tomb."

"Thank you. I need spiritual guidance, protection, and prayer."

"I can relate, Ntsayi. One can't afford to relax around here with evil forces at work plotting one's failure."

We continued walking and arrived at the Kizinga, which wasn't yet open for prayer. Ntsayi knocked on the door, and a teenager came out. He invited us inside, motioned to a wooden bench, and said, "Please, take a seat."

He pulled a chair from the table and sat in front of us. *This boy is certainly not the Moumbikoudi Ntsayi came to see,* I thought. He looked at both Ntsayi and me inquiringly and said, "Close your eyes and let's pray."

Suddenly, the Moumbikoudi got into a trance, turned his attention to me. He then prophesied in these words: "If you want to pass the baccalaureate exam, you'd better move out of your house," said the spirit of God.

The Moumbikoudi told us to open our eyes. He paused and spoke in tongues, gesturing with his hands, and said, "I can see through my eyes of faith that evil forces are at work, plotting your failure."

He paused for a second, stood up from his chair, looked right through me, placed his left hand on his chest, raised his right hand toward the sky, spoke in tongues for a minute, and continued, "These are the same evil forces that caused your older sister Judith to twice fail her baccalaureate exam. The spirit of God reveals that your sister is a bright young lady and is a hardworking student like you. But there are evil forces operating in your family; they're determined to hinder your success."

He paused again and spoke in tongues. I was hanging on his every word, eager to find out the truth. He then said, "But fear not, my brother. God is on your side. I believe it's no coincidence Ntsayi asked you to come with him. The Almighty wants to deliver you and your siblings from the spells of those evil forces."

I was confused trying to make sense of his revelations. *Is this true? I can't take everything this teenager says at face value, can I? How did he know my sister's name and details about her life?* I wondered.

He prayed in tongues again, prophesied over Ntsayi, and concluded the prayer session. We thanked the man of God and left the Kizinga.

"What do you think? Huh? Weren't his revelations spot-on?" Ntsayi enthused.

"Yes, indeed! I now have some tough decisions to make."

"Me too. Lazare, everything will work out for the best, you'll see."

I meditated on the Moumbikoudi's insightful revelations after Ntsayi and I had said goodbye. *I have to act fast; time is of the essence*, I thought. It was because of these factors I decided to move out against my father's wishes.

On Saturday morning in March 1998, I packed all my clothes in a duffle bag, squeezed all my books inside my school backpack, and walked out of the door. My father looked his normal self as he was standing in the front yard next to our well.

"Come to my tailor shop for school fees and any other expenses. Understood?"

"Yes, Dad! Tié-Tié is close from there."

My father pulled some money out of his pocket and handed it to me, saying, "This is for your taxi fare and pocket money for the week. Be good!"

I said goodbye to my siblings, walked to the corner of Avenue de la Liberté, stopped in front of Grand Omar's food shop, hailed a Toyota Hiace van taxi, climbed into the back seat, and the driver asked, "Where to?"

"OCH," I replied.

Noko Loussoukou and his family made me feel at home right away.

"You can share this room with your cousin Will," Noko Loussoukou said.

Will looked excited, his face beaming with a smile. He shook my hand and showed me where to put my stuff. My cousins and I got along very well. All of them were either in their first or second year of high school. I was amongst like-minded people in a much quieter environment. I set up a study group with four hardworking, self-disciplined, and brilliant classmates. During those six months, all my focus was on my studies. I would get up at 4am daily, sit on the front porch, and study. After school in the late afternoon, I would study some more with my classmates. In the evening, I would go to a Kizinga to attend prayer sessions. The day of the exam in August 1998 I was more than ready to rise to the challenge. This was the moment I was studying hard for. I was majoring in French literature and foreign languages. I wrote what I believed to be a bulletproof paper for French and Philosophy. I answered most questions correctly for Spanish, English, and history and geography. I did okay in my physical training test. Overall, I felt confident and good about my chances of success.

THE VERDICT

After two months had gone by, it was announced on the late evening news on national television that the results for the baccalaureate exam were ready. The announcer spoke about the statistics, which didn't look good. He highlighted how the success rate had dramatically dropped this year compared to the year before. The news made me doubt my chances of success. I couldn't sleep well; I tossed and turned in bed and kept wondering what I would do if I failed.

Early in the morning, I turned on the radio and patiently listened to every boring program until they started reading the results per region and per high school. Out of a thousand candidates in Pointe-Noire 2, only 166 students passed. When I heard my name, I leapt off the front porch, punching the air in celebration and shouting, "Yes! I made it!" Noko Loussoukou, his wife, and my cousins congratulated and rejoiced with me.

"You should stay here until you go to Brazzaville for enrollment," Noko Loussoukou said.

"I can't make such a decision without involving my dad," I replied.

"Fair enough. Talk to your dad about it. I would love to have you continue living here with us."

"I'll let him know. I'm going to Tié-Tié at once to tell him the good news," I enthused.

"I'm going to university," I exclaimed to myself in excitement. I felt so relieved that my hard work, self-discipline, and decision to go against my father's wishes had paid off. I felt confident that my life was about to unfold exactly how I expected it to. My sights were now set on Brazzaville. I got ready and rushed to my father's tailor shop. I walked fast in Pointe-Noire's usual heat and was sweating and panting when I got there. My father and his two employees were seated behind their pedal Singer classic sewing machines, tailoring away. Upon seeing me, my father stopped pedaling, smiled, stood up, and came to give me a big hug.

"I'm proud of you, son. Congratulations!" my father said with a big smile on his face.

"Thank you, Dad," I said, my face gleaming with joy.

"If you consistently maintain the same work rate, I have no doubt in my mind you'll achieve great things. Remember, you have my full support!"

"I appreciate it, Dad."

My father's words of praise and encouragement filled me with confidence and ineffable joy. I felt as if I had the world under my feet and the sky was the limit. I was a little scared but still thrilled at the prospect of studying law at University Marien Ngouabi. My father then told me to return home immediately.

"Noko Loussoukou suggested that I continue staying with them," I said.

"You already know the answer to that," my father smirked.

I went back to OCH, packed my belongings, and headed straight back to Voungou. I could not contain my joy; I ran to Ntsayi's place, who also was celebrating, and I joined in.

"Will you also be going to Brazzaville?" I asked Ntsayi.

"No, I don't want to. Remember the trip I confided to you about?"

"Oh! Yes, I remember. Is your dad going to help you?"

"Sort of. You know the small businesses I've been running since high school?"

"Yes, I know. You told me about it a few times before."

"Well, I've been saving up money. I've saved up enough for my ticket fare and for the first year's tuition."

"Wow! That's amazing, Ntsayi!"

"Thank you, Lazare! My dad promised to help me with rent and will be sending me pocket money monthly. But once I'm there, I'll find a part-time job. I already have a few connections in Paris."

I left Ntsayi's place after we celebrated and conversed for a while and went back to my place, where there was more rejoicing with my siblings.

PLANNING FOR UNIVERSITY

The sun was shining bright; it was scorching but glorious. My elder sister Judith and I were standing in the shade of the mango tree in the middle of our front yard, chatting away. Judith teased me about the challenges that would face me once I got to Brazzaville.

"You need a new look to impress the ladies at university, little brother!" Judith teased with a broad smile on her face.

"What do you know, anyway? I won't change anything to please anyone, trust me, sister," I giggled.

"Senior students enjoy making fun of freshmen," she teased.

I had heard lots of stories about how senior students treated freshmen, but I never took them at face value. With my hands in my pocket, my head held up high, my shoulders back, a smile on my face, I said, "I'll be the first freshman nobody will mess with."

"Don't flatter yourself, young brother," she burst out laughing.

"I stand by my statement. I'll let nobody ridicule or bully me."

"Every freshman speaks with confidence like you before they go to Marien Ngouabi."

"I won't lose any sleep over it," I yawned.

Judith stopped giving me grief about university when our father walked up to where we were standing and joking around. I couldn't read him because when quiet, he always looked serious.

"Son, would you be interested in purchasing some fabrics here to sell in Mouyondzi?" he started.

Before I could answer, Judith interjected, "How can you even think that, Dad?"

"Your brother has so much free time on his hands before university starts," he said.

"Which he should use to rest and prepare for university," she emphasized.

He paused for a second, turned to look Judith in the eye. With authority in his voice, he ordered, "Stop interrupting me, Judith!"

"But Dad, this is a terrible idea!" she whined.

"How would you know? Huh?" he asked, sounding annoyed.

Judith didn't answer. She threw her hands in the air in frustration and shook her head to stress her opposition to the idea. I didn't intervene because I wanted to find out more about my father's plan.

"As I was trying to say before your sister here interrupted me," he shot her a quick look and turned his attention back to me, "would you be interested in purchasing fabrics here to sell in Mouyondzi?"

"I don't know, Dad," I said. I darted a glance at Judith, who shook her head, trying to tell me not to do it. I looked back at my dad and focused.

"A quick trip to Mouyondzi will help you kill two birds with one stone."

"What do you mean, Dad?"

"You'll spend time with your mother, visit the rest of the family in Mouyondzi, and sell the fabrics while you're there," he explained with a little smile on his face, sounding positive about the whole plan.

"I still don't know how I feel about this, Dad."

"Look at it this way. The money you make from those sales will help pay for your tuition."

"So will I be able to keep some of it?"

"Of course, yes."

"Dad, don't send him there, please," Judith said.

"This is a quick business trip. Don't worry! Your brother won't stay there long. He'll be back here with us in less than three weeks."

"People have been complaining about safety issues when traveling anywhere by train these days."

"Judith, your brother will be fine."

"Dad, things can easily take a turn for the worse."

"Judith, stop worrying! Your brother will be fine!"

"You can't guarantee that, Dad," she said.

I thought Judith's protest to our father's idea made sense. However, the excitement of seeing my mother, little sister, and the rest of my extended family outweighed any indecision I had about taking a trip to Mouyondzi. Judith gave up trying to persuade our father not to follow through with his plan. My dad and I went to the factory shop and purchased the merchandise. We were both in high spirits. I was now looking forward to making the trip. There was positive energy all around. Plus, the sun was shining, the sky was blue, and there was a cool breeze blowing. The day was gorgeous.

"Son, you go to Mouyondzi, sell the fabrics, and hop back on the train as soon as possible. Don't stay there longer than you have to."

"Dad, as you already know, I've never done this before."

"You have nothing to worry about, son."

"Okay!" I said, nodding in agreement.

"Ndazet has been running his own grocery store in Mouyondzi for years. He has a lot of connections and loads of experience in business. He'll help you sell the merchandise. You'll be back here in no time."

"All right, Dad, consider it done."

ON MY WAY TO MOUYONDZI

The wooden clock hanging above the giant entrance of the main train station in Pointe-Noire read 5:00 pm. The main train station is an old, worn-out building the Republic of Congo inherited from the colonists. The building has been deprived of genuine maintenance since colonization. The whole structure is in such a precarious condition that it is clearly a disaster waiting to happen.

From the first second I got out of the taxi, I felt as if I was willingly walking into a lion's den.

"Get in line!" a soldier ordered.

I stood in line and waited for my turn. I approached the kiosk, handed the ticket agent the money, and said, "One way ticket to Bouansa, please."

She didn't say anything, nodded, took the money, slid it into the cash drawer, and handed me the ticket. I glanced at it, shoved it into my pocket, hesitated, and thought I needed to reserve a good seat.

"Oh! Sorry! Is it possible to reserve a seat?" I asked.

"Of course, yes. You have to pay an additional fee for it," the ticket agent said.

"How much is it?"

"500 Franc CFA, please," she replied.

I paid for my ticket and the additional fee. I had to present it to the soldiers, who stood before the checkpoint. One of them took a glance at it and waved me through the checkpoint, motioning me to proceed straight to the platform. I strode through the rusty steel gate that led to the station's only platform. I stepped onto the platform and couldn't believe my eyes. There were too many people everywhere, and all were impatiently waiting for the same train. I thought to myself, *It's mathematically impossible for everybody to fit into a ten-coach train. There's absolutely not enough room for everybody here.* The sad part was, if one missed the train, there was no refund and disputing it would be a total waste of time and energy. I began worrying about whether I could make it or not. I nudged my way through what looked like an impenetrable crowd of boisterous people and soldiers and sat on my luggage. The train was scheduled to depart from Pointe-Noire's station at 6 pm. Three hours had elapsed when the train slowly rolled into the station. With all my strength, I had to muscle my way into a coach. There was no queue or any form of organized system to facilitate a smooth and painless boarding process. It was literally organized chaos. I got pushed around like everybody else, trodden on, insulted in the process, but I stood my ground. I felt that it was only a test to prove to myself that I was man enough.

"You're hurting my arm," somebody cried.

"Get out of my fucking way," a soldier shouted.

"You're suffocating me!" a woman lamented.

"Watch out, hot water coming," a young man screamed, trying to trick his way onto the train before anybody else.

Through the organized chaos, I miraculously found myself on board the train. I was disappointed to see that soldiers occupied all the seats. These soldiers were duty bound to protect the passengers.

"If you want a seat, step into my office and pay me for it!" a soldier advertised.

He looked around and waited a second to see whether somebody was interested in the deal. All civilian passengers were quiet, looked afraid, and tried to avoid eye contact with him.

"Only cash please, no checks allowed," he smirked.

I became aware of the tense, stressful, and depressing post-civil war atmosphere in my country. So I didn't dare open my mouth to the soldier who rested in the seat I had reserved and paid for beforehand. My money was gone.

The train was jam-packed and it was overflowing with passengers, luggage, and merchandise. I couldn't believe my eyes. There were people and merchandise hanging, dangling, or perched on almost every compartment of the train. We looked like a colony of hungry ants trying to devour a dead cricket. It felt exhausting and very stressful to say the least. I tightened my grip on my luggage. I had the delicate mission to guard it with my life. We had waited three hours before the train arrived in the station. Two more hours later we heard the whistle, and the train began to slowly roll away from the station. There were even more travelers sprinting after it, trying to get on.

In our coach, there was a young soldier in his early twenties, a new recruit, who went by the name Beretta. He stood about 5'7 inches tall and looked stocky, strong, and bellicose. He took the luxury of occupying four seats in a fully-packed train. He sold two of his seats and held on to two. He guarded his private space like an eagle with perfect peripheral vision and wouldn't let anybody go anywhere near it. He almost came to blows with another soldier in the coach.

"Why can't you let this old man sit?" the soldier asked.

Beretta sprang to his feet. He looked angry, with his fists clenched, and was standing face to face with his fellow soldier.

"Mind your own bloody business!" Beretta said.

"Who on earth do you think you are?" his fellow soldier replied.

Tension was mounting and I could feel the temperature in the coach rise to 120 degrees. Both soldiers looked evenly matched, and neither one of them showed any sign of backing down. A fight between soldiers on the train was the last thing anybody wanted to witness. Unfortunately, civilian passengers couldn't intervene to try and pacify the situation. It was a military affair.

"If you want drama, I'm going to give you drama. I won't

hesitate to detonate this grenade, and let it blow up this bloody coach!" he said.

"You're bluffing! There's nothing you can do!" his fellow soldier said.

Beretta took two steps back, unbuckled the grenade from his belt, and threatened, "Try me, maggot! I can blow up this bloody coach right now!"

At that point we all held our breath and silently prayed that he wouldn't blow up the coach. Other soldiers had to step in to pacify the situation. It was unfortunate for the population that many of these new army recruits were illiterate, school dropouts, kleptomaniacs, bandits, or people who had no regard for human rights. Sadly, the army was in need of personnel. So they were recruiting almost anybody.

The train moved at a very slow pace, like an African leopard tortoise. We were about two hundred kilometers from Bouansa and had traveled for twelve hours to get there. For twelve long hours I had to listen to soldiers scream profanities at civilian passengers; I had to watch them perform "legal theft" and treat passengers badly without apparent reason. During the trip, I stayed silent, motionless, and almost catatonic. I didn't want to get into an argument with anybody. I was trying to reach my destination unharmed. The train finally screeched to a halt at Bouansa station, and as I began to shoot for the exit, I felt an unusual force pulling my luggage. I turned around and found myself face to face with Beretta. He was staring into my eyes; I felt unlucky that our paths had crossed. Right there, I regretted agreeing to make the trip. I had to both man up and wise up to find a way to emerge unscathed from this predicament.

"What's inside the fucking bag?" he shouted.

His tone of voice was condescending, rude, and abusive. He acted as if he had been insulted. Beretta was ready to strike again. This time, I was his unfortunate victim.

"Open the fucking bag, right now!" Beretta angrily barked like a wild dog ready to pounce on his prey.

I hesitated and stumbled over my words in a desperate attempt to explain myself to him.

"I'm trying to…and…" I stammered.

"Shut your bloody mouth!" he interjected.

I could neither gather my thoughts nor form a sentence. He wouldn't give me a chance and kept on interrupting and barking insults at me.

"You maggot!" he shouted.

I tried ignoring his abuse and was fumbling with the zipper of my bag. Suddenly, he snatched the bag of fabrics out of my grip and unzipped it with so much force that the zipper nearly broke off. At that moment, I wish he'd suffer a heart attack or be struck by lightning; I wished all sorts of evil on him. He reached inside my bag and pulled out some of the fabrics I was carrying. I felt paralyzing fury rise from the pit of my stomach to every cell in my body. Despite this paralyzing fury boiling within me, I remained calm by reminding myself how fast and easily I could get hurt or killed if I tried to challenge him. So I composed myself and tried to keep my answers to his questions monotone. I let him dramatize the situation to satisfy his self-inflated ego and waited for the opportune time to bribe my way out of the situation. I had to think and act fast because trains stopped at every station for only ten minutes. I could not afford to miss my stop.

"Who the hell do you think you are, asshole?" he stormed.

"I-I'm…am…" I stuttered.

"Where the fuck are you going?

"I'm on my way to…to…" I stammered.

"Where is your fucking ticket, blockhead?"

"I have it somewhere in my jacket," I replied in a shaky voice.

"Show me your fucking ticket right now!" he barked.

I reached into the inside pocket of the jacket I was wearing and presented my ticket to him. He snatched it out of my right hand, glanced at it, and shoved it down his trousers' back pocket.

"Where is your bloody permit for these goods?"

I looked at him, surprised, since I had no idea what he was

talking about. I knew what he was looking for but I still had to play it by ear to figure out how to proceed.

"I don't have a permit, and I didn't know I needed one," I blurted.

"Shut up and show me your bloody permit, motherfucker!"

"Sorry, I don't have one," I said.

The other soldiers in our coach didn't even attempt to stop their comrade, who clearly was out of line. They didn't care and were just conversing as if nothing was happening. This was frustrating to see because their main mission was to keep passengers like me safe. My fellow civilian passengers looked scandalized and were looking at me with compassion and empathy in their eyes. There was no such thing as a permit for carrying goods on the train. Everybody carried all types of goods with them all the time. There were no rules that prohibited passengers from carrying merchandise on the train. Unlike some passengers who sell stuff on the train, I wasn't trying to sell anyone anything. He was looking for an excuse to confiscate my merchandise; this was nothing else but daylight robbery.

"Get the hell out of my sight!" He waved me away.

I had to stay calm, play along, and submit to his authority to avoid losing my merchandise. I stayed rooted in the same spot as he rambled on about his influence, authority, and power.

"This is my fucking train! I make the rules, and you motherfuckers have got to abide by them! I put my life on the line to liberate you cowards from a dictatorial regime! I'm your fucking hero! Yeah! That's fucking right! You mess with me, you mess with the law!" he said.

The train was getting ready to leave Bouansa. Thus, I wasted no more time, reached down in my socks to retrieve the only cash I had left, and paid Beretta for breaking a set of unwritten rules and regulations that seemed to govern the new Congo. He then flung the luggage back at me and kicked me out of the coach. He concluded the whole experience by spewing out more verbal abuse at me.

"Fuck off and get the hell out of here, maggot!"

My luggage flew over my head as my chest heavily hit the dusty ground. I was momentarily enveloped in a cloud of yellowish dust. I stood up quickly, grabbed my luggage, dusted myself off, and walked toward the taxis going to Mouyondzi.

We reap what we sow. Everybody pays for what they do to others eventually, I thought. Bouansa was buzzing, people were milling about, ambulant salesmen and saleswomen were hustling for customers, and business was in full swing everywhere. The aroma of fruits, fermented yucca, bush meat, and other types of goods filled the air. The sun had majestically risen above the blue sky, diffusing its pure rays of light across the land. It was just beginning to get warm. I removed the jacket I had been wearing and stuffed it into my bag. I was ready to continue my journey. But after the incident in the train, I didn't have any money left to afford taxi fare for the trip to Mouyondzi. I began thinking about how vehemently opposed to this trip Judith was.

"If only I had listened to Judith, none of this would be happening right now. Why did I agree to make the trip?" I muttered.

I could imagine Judith confronting Dad about the whole plan. There I was, with no money, stranded at a train station where I knew nobody. I had to man up and wise up to figure out how to address the pickle I found myself in. I was prepared to beg or liquidate the fabrics at ridiculously low prices to make money for the last part of my trip. "I'll exhaust every option and as a last resort, if all fails, I'll then liquidate the fabrics," I muttered. I mustered up some courage and approached a friendly-looking taxi driver to ask for help. He was crouched behind his vehicle and looked busy, maybe trying to repair something or tighten a loose screw.

"Excuse me, sir?" I said.

"What can I do for you?" he asked in a friendly tone of voice.

"Sorry to interrupt… I…uh…" I stammered.

"How can I help?" he asked.

He didn't turn around to look at me as he continued working on his vehicle.

"I was just wondering, uh, if you could, uh, could, d-do me a favor…" I stuttered.

"A favor, you say?"

He stood up, turned around to look at me, pulled a handkerchief out of his khaki shorts, and wiped sweat off his brow and the grease off his hands.

"I'm on my way to Nkila-poste," I confided.

He looked at me from head to toe and exclaimed, sounding sympathetic, "You look like hell!"

"Correct! I look like hell because I have just been through hell on the train," I said.

"Is that so? What went wrong, brother?"

"I was unfortunate enough to lose my money to a crooked soldier. All this happened as I was about to get off the train," I explained.

I felt physically and mentally exhausted. I set my bag on the dusty ground, interlaced my fingers for a second, rubbed my brow, scratched the back of my head, stretched my neck, looked down, and put my hands in my pockets.

"I'm sorry to hear that."

"Thank you for listening to my story," I said.

I looked lost and confused, which my interlocutor picked up on. He then asked, "Have you ever been to this part of the country before?"

"Yes, I have but it was a very long time ago," I replied.

"Whereabouts in Nkila-poste are you going, brother?"

"I'm going to my uncle's, Ndazet, the small grocery store owner near Nkila-poste center."

"Oh, you're Ndazet's nephew? I know him well; he is a friend," he grinned.

"He is my dad's younger brother!" I enthused.

"I can drop you off there. The ancestors are certainly with you. Welcome to Mouyondzi, brother!"

Dad was right about Papa Ndazet having a lot of connections, I thought. One of his connections was about to save my life. So I began to feel buoyant about the prospect of selling the fabrics quickly and returning to Pointe-Noire in no time. I expressed my gratitude to the Good Samaritan and asked for his name. "Sorry, I didn't get your name."

"Call me Milanze. You can get in the car. We're leaving soon," he chuckled.

"I truly appreciate your help, Milanze."

"Don't mention it," Milanze said.

I felt relieved that Milanze was willing to drive me to my destination free of charge. Plus, he radiated so much positive energy that conversing with him helped lift up my spirits. I climbed into the back seat of his van, which was almost full. Off we went on a long and bumpy ride, which I quite enjoyed, to be honest. The van tires screeched on the clay ground and lifted a cloud of dust behind us as the driver raced the vehicle away. Fifty kilometers of dirt and gravel road, edged by lush vegetation, stood between Bouansa train station and Mouyondzi. The view of nature was awesome and majestic. The fauna and flora looked so pristine that it would have inspired a fine work of art. The vehicle passed tiny villages consisting of circular, square, and rectangular mud houses with thatched roofs built along riverbanks, near forests, or behind hills and mountains. Villagers with broad smiles on their faces stood on the side of the road and waved to passengers. Milanze expertly raced the vehicle through a winding side road, stopped at two villages, dropped off three passengers, and picked up some more on the way back. We traveled a few more kilometers until Nkila-poste came into full view. The vehicle gradually reduced speed and its tires screeched to a halt in front of Papa Ndazet's store. "Enjoy your stay in Mouyondzi, young brother!" Milanze said as he revved the van's engine and drove away.

THE INCEPTION OF THE REBELLION

No sooner did I set foot in Mouyondzi than machine guns started thundering and rattling across the village. Everyone fell flat on the ground to dodge a wave of bullets tearing through the air like flashes of lightning, slicing branches off trees, piercing through brick walls, shattering glass windows and doors, and wreaking havoc at an alarming speed. Sounds of distress arose from all directions: mothers crying for their children, fathers ordering everybody to run for cover. Every living creature went into survival mode.

"Get down! Get down on the floor now!" somebody frantically motioned.

"Where is my child?" a woman in panic mode cried.

"Get inside the house now!" a man barked instructions at his kids.

In the middle of this chaos, gunshots continued to rattle defiantly and echo across the entire district. With my hands clasped around my head, I began to perspire like somebody in a steam bath. I stayed hidden behind banana trees growing near Papa Ndazet's grocery store. I could hear my heart throb in my head and feel my insides tense up each time a stray bullet whistled past my hiding spot. Time stood still. I was both afraid and confused. My whole body was shaking uncontrollably. My brain was drawing a blank. I was struggling to figure out what to do. I cursed the day I came into this world and blamed my father for it. "Why was I born? I wish I were never born. Shame on you, Dad!" I muttered. I wished the whole situation were just a nightmare I could easily snap out of. Unfortunately, I was there witnessing the entire volatile situation unraveling. Tears welled up in my eyes as I strove to comprehend the string of misfortunes that seemed to stalk me everywhere I went. On that day, it looked as though the sun refused to set. The shooting frenzy stopped as abruptly as it commenced. I carefully poked my head out of my hiding spot, peeked around my surroundings, and surmised that it looked safe enough to venture out. I slowly rose to my feet and stumbled my way to the front of Papa Ndazet's store, where I saw everybody heading to the Mbongui.

"Where is everybody going?" I asked.

"To the Mbongui to find out what's really going on," a bystander replied.

I joined the people walking and we all ended up at the Mbongui, where a middle-aged gentleman on an elevated platform towering over everybody was addressing the crowd. He looked wise, was well spoken, the deep tone of his voice commanding authority and respect. The audience hung on his every word.

"Dear inhabitants of Mouyondzi, there is nothing to be alarmed about! Fear not because everything is under control. The shooting you heard earlier was from our soldiers taking control of the entire district," he declared. He paused for a second, looked around the audience, removed his reading glasses, rubbed his eyes, cleared his throat, and continued his elocution. "We, the civil servants, hereby vehemently refuse to serve an administration that usurped power, an administration whose methods are opposed to democracy, an administration that conquered the country by means of a civil war. So we say no to dictatorship and viva the rebellion!" he announced with his right fist raised.

A round of applause followed, but there were still mixed feelings and reactions in the audience. Some were uneasy, confused, and unsure, whereas others felt that rebelling against the new administration was the right thing to do. In an attempt to initiate national reconciliation and rebuild the country, the new administration had formally mandated all civil servants to return to work. But rebels threatened to kill anybody who dared return to work. They tried everything in their power to hinder the reconciliation. So the new administration had the daunting task of restoring law and order in some of the violence-stricken regions of the south. Therefore, the new administration vowed to meet force with force and slay anybody who would dare to stand in its way. The shooting frenzy that welcomed my arrival in Mouyondzi marked the beginning of a long period of uncertainty. Most inhabitants decided to rise up against the new administration. One needed nerves of steel not to lose their composure. Papa Ndazet couldn't hide his frustration about my presence there. I empathized with him, considering the circumstances. He was standing by the door of his grocery store, his arms crossed and resting on his chest, and frustration was written all over his face.

"Why on earth did your father send you here?" he stormed.

I was sitting on a wooden bench next to where he was standing, rubbing my eyes, scratching my head, and looking as anxious as everybody else. I tried to avoid eye contact with him and calmly replied, "Father, I'm at the right place at the wrong time."

"Right place at the wrong time, huh? Didn't you hear the rumors of an impending war in Mouyondzi?" he asked.

"I vaguely heard something, but I didn't read too much into it," I blurted in a subdued tone.

"If you paid a little more attention, you wouldn't have come to Mouyondzi!" he almost shouted, gesturing with his hands in frustration.

"Are we not blowing everything out of proportion, father?" I asked.

The question got him more riled up. He looked me in the eye and emphasized, "This is not a nightmare one struggles to wake from. This is reality! People will be brutally killed! Do you understand that?"

"Yes sir, I do," I said.

"Welcome to Mouyondzi!" he exclaimed and walked away.

I knew that he was absolutely right. But being right didn't change anything. The whole conversation made me think more about the situation. I tried to process the gravity of what was about to happen before my eyes. I had more questions than answers. I felt both confused and unsure about what my next move was going to be. Suddenly, the thought of returning to Pointe-Noire lingered in my head. It looked as though there was one way in and no way out. The sun gradually disappeared behind the sky, and nightfall came upon us like a savior. I could finally lie down, go to sleep, and put all my worries and fears aside, at least for a while. The next morning, the sun rose majestically above the sky in its splendor and a new day began. There was a glimmer of hope in my heart for the restoration of peace to the country. Little did I know that bigger trouble was brewing in the background and the future looked rather bleak. The rebellion was real and there was nothing anybody could do to stop it.

CONQUERING MOUYONDZI

The rebels launched their first attack on Mouyondzi. The few government forces dispersed across the district were caught by surprise. Some managed to miraculously escape but others weren't so lucky. The rebels conquered the whole district in no time and got more weapons and ammunition from the government forces' arsenal. They took control of the country's main power plant in Moukoukoulou and captured the Rwandese soldiers that were tasked with securing it. Kimpoungou took it upon himself to interrogate the prisoners. He stroked his joint of weed with his steel-like fingers, placed it between his fat and dark lips, and lit it up. He puffed on his joint a few times and blew out smoke all over the prisoners' subdued-looking faces.

"Are you having fun yet?" he scoffed.

He puffed on his joint some more, put it out, and flicked it away. He then looked at the prisoners intently, without saying a word, and spat on the floor in disgust. He took off his woolen sweater, drenched with sweat, and flung it at one of the prisoners, who instinctively ducked. He approached the prisoner, looked him up and down, and suddenly grabbed him by the throat. The prisoner tried to wiggle free, shrieking with pain, but Kimpoungou tightened his grip, trying to choke him to death, then released him, saying, "I'm just getting started," he paused, "worthless sons of bitches!"

He then took two steps back and crouched beside a rock he used as a file. He sharpened his axe and machete, stripped the prisoners of their military uniforms, and tied their naked bodies with barbed wires to the palm trees.

"Don't you try to move, motherfuckers! You're my fucking puppets! I pull the strings, you dance," he smirked.

He tightened the barbed wires around the prisoners' wrists and ankles. The barbed wires pricked their limbs, causing them to yelp in pain, and there was a trickle of blood.

"What is your story, ugly face, huh?" he laughed.

One of the prisoners, with tears in his eyes, started begging for mercy in a foreign dialect, which seemed to amuse Kimpoungou. He laughed hysterically, waving his axe in the air in a sign of triumph. He suddenly stopped laughing and shouted, "Shut the fuck up!" The prisoner flinched, sniffled, and fell silent.

The two other prisoners looked at the crowd. Their eyelids flickered as their eyes begged for mercy. They drew compassion from some people in the audience, who struggled to blink back their tears and left the scene immediately. Kimpoungou rolled a second joint, lit it, took a few puffs, blew out smoke through his nose, and paused. He puffed on it one more time, held his breath for a nanosecond, and blew out smoke over the prisoners' faces, who blinked. Kimpoungou took one step back, flicked the rest of his joint away and suddenly looked nostalgic as he reminisced about the horrors he'd witnessed in Brazzaville.

> *"A pool of blood on the floor—*
> *He looked round, glanced at the door*
> *Riddled with bullet holes,*
> *Swaying through two giant poles.*
>
> *He dashed into the house,*
> *Saw a naked body mourning for his head.*
> *The gruesome scene gave him no time to muse.*
> *In the background, machine guns rumbled.*

He tumbled down in shock and passed out.
For a few seconds he battled to rise
Until a grenade thundered through the house;
He sprang back to his feet and sped toward the exit,

Zooming past corpses and dead bodies.
A hellish rage seized his bowels
As his mind replayed the gory scenes.
He swore to avenge his loved ones."

He started pacing back and forth before the prisoners, and then stopped, ominously staring at them for less than a minute. He clutched his axe with both hands and briskly swung it across the neck of the prisoner closest to him. The prisoner's head swiftly parted from its neck, bounced off a rock, rolled across the green grass like a soccer ball, and finally bit the dust. A fountain of blood spurted out of the prisoner's headless body, staining his hands, chiseled torso, and strong-looking biceps. Kimpoungou leapt around with joy, like a little boy with a new toy.

"Oh yes! That's how you crush your enemies! That was great fun!" he enthused.

Kimpoungou laughed hysterically, jumping around, punching the air, like somebody who'd just hit the jackpot. The two remaining prisoners began to tremble uncontrollably. They glanced at their compatriot's lifeless, decapitated body lying in his own pool of blood and tears were streaming down their faces. Suddenly, they started slurring words in their dialect, maybe begging for mercy, which seemed to amuse Kimpoungou, his six-foot tall figure towering over them.

"Fucking mercenaries, begging for mercy? You're trained killers, for God's sake!" he scoffed.

Everybody in the audience looked on in utter shock and horror. He bent down, picked up a military uniform he'd confiscated from the prisoners earlier, and wiped the blood off his body with it. He looked straight into the prisoners' eyes and shook his head in disbelief. "You cowards are fucking hilarious!" he scoffed. He paced back and forth, looking pensive, stroking his beardless chin, and suddenly stopped.

"Which one of the two of you wants to die next, huh?" he asked.

Both prisoners looked resigned to their fate and stopped begging for mercy. Kimpoungou reached for his machete lying beside the rock, pressed his right knee against one of the two prisoners' loins, placed his left hand firmly on the prisoner's mouth, and with the right vigorously drove the machete into his stomach. The moribund prisoner twisted and curled in agony until he gave up the ghost. Kimpoungou's hands were soaked in blood. He wore an evil look on his face, his bulging eyes looking like they were about to pop out of their sockets. He was having the time of his life.

"Revenge is sweet! I take great pleasure in annihilating my enemies!" he said.

The last prisoner poured out a torrent of tears and soiled himself. All those horrified by the gory scene quickly got away from there. Kimpoungou dropped his weapon of choice on the ground and turned to look at the audience, and some people stumbled backwards. Kimpoungou raised his right hand and said, "Don't be afraid!"

Still in shock, the audience was transfixed and looked as if Kimpoungou had hypnotized or put them under some sort of spell.

"These sons of bitches are cold-blooded killers! Do not pity them!" he cursed.

Kimpoungou paced back and forth in front of the dead bodies with pride, showing no remorse for his actions.

"These fucking mercenaries dug their own graves a long time ago when they set foot in this country," he boasted. He paused for a second to gather his thoughts and clarified, "They're paid by those who lust for power to take innocent lives, to kill innocent people like you and me. They're mercenaries, born killers!"

Who has the right to take another human being's life? Are we not all destined to die some day? I suppose Kimpoungou and every killer believe they're immortal, I thought.

"I need a volunteer to send this bloodsucking leech to hell," he said.

Everybody at the scene turned around, murmuring, and looked at one another in utter shock. The audience began to thin out.

With the machete in his right hand, he gestured triumphantly, waving it in the air, and asked, "Who is brave enough to come and put this fucking mercenary out of his misery?"

The crowd, now thunderstruck, continued to stare at Kimpoungou in disbelief.

"Don't let me finish this party all by myself," he smirked.

He paused momentarily and paced back and forth with his hand cupped on his chin, lost in his thoughts. Suddenly, he stopped and turned toward the crowd to address them one more time.

"Mouyondzi is the land of the brave! I need a volunteer to end this killer's miserable life!"

A thirteen-year-old boy appeared out of nowhere, stepped forward, and strode toward Kimpoungou. Kimpoungou looked around the crowd with a smirk on his face and made a sign with his thumb to signal his satisfaction. He then put his left hand on the boy's shoulder, knelt on one knee so he was face to face with the boy, looked him in the eye, and like a loving father addressing his favorite child, he asked, "What is your name, lion heart? And how old are you, mighty warrior?"

"My name is Ntsende and I'm thirteen years old," the boy emotionlessly replied.

"Are you sure that you want to do this?" Kimpoungou nicely asked the boy.

At first, everybody thought it was a joke when they saw the boy pick up the machete. He then took a step closer to the prisoner, swung it and whacked him to death. A pool of blood oozed out of the prisoner's wounded body as he met his maker. Ntsende's clothes, hands, feet, and face were stained with the victim's blood. His body trembled as if caught in a trance of some sort. Kimpoungou gently removed the machete from Ntsende's grip and set it on the ground. He gave Ntsende a warm, brotherly embrace and praised him for his bravery.

"You did good, son! You're the man, kid!" Kimpoungou said.

The gory scene left people utterly horrified and shocked, to say the least, earning both Ntsende and Kimpoungou some notoriety across Mouyondzi. Kimpoungou took Ntsende under his wing and made him his right-hand man. Ntsende idolized him, learned from him, and continued developing under his tutelage.

The rebellion enabled anarchy to take root in Mouyondzi. The rebels dismantled the institutions that once governed the district. The volatile situation started spawning interesting characters everywhere, and Mbingou fit the profile. He kidnapped a poor lady and held her captive.

"Your government took everything from me. They left me with nothing!"

"I have no idea what you're talking about, but I'm really sorry."

"Sorry, huh? The civil war in Brazzaville—does it ring a bell?"

"I'm sorry. I wasn't even in Brazzaville during the civil war."

"Liar! You people from the north persecuted us out of Brazzaville!"

"Please, let me go! I had nothing to do with the civil war."

Mbingou looked the lady up and down, made a face to express his disgust and said, "My shoe repair shop got pillaged. If I hadn't escaped from there, I would have been savagely beaten and brutally murdered by your soldiers. And you expect me to let you go?"

"I'm truly sorry to hear it. Yes, I'm from the north but I'm just a simple civil servant. Please, let me go, I'm begging you."

"Huh? Absolute nonsense! You expect me to believe that?"

"Neither my family nor I had anything to do with the civil war," she explained.

"You're a lying bitch!" he yelled.

The shouting and yelling drew passers by to Mbingou's parents' property, and a crowd began to form.

"Please, let the poor lady go!" some people pleaded.

He turned around to face the crowd and asked, "Huh? Why would I let her go?"

"She's been a high school teacher here for a long time," somebody explained.

"Yes, she is teacher and I can testify to that!" another person confirmed.

Soon everybody in the crowd was shouting in unison, "Let her go!" Mbingou fired shots in the air with his AK47, causing most people to bolt. He then addressed the few who defiantly wouldn't move.

"If any of you tries to get involved again, I won't hesitate to pull the trigger," he threatened, waving his gun at them. They finally moved farther from the scene. Mbingou set his gun on the ground beside a wooden bench and sat down in front of his captive. He lit up his Tumbaco Leggere cigarette, puffed on it contentedly, and gently put it in an ashtray that rested on a dry tree trunk.

He opened his bottle of palm wine, took a sip, smiled, and said, "Do you want some?" His captive shook her head no. He rolled his eyes in surprise and said, "Your loss."

He took another sip of his Ntsamba and set the bottle down; he picked up his cigarette, repeatedly puffed on it and coughed out smoke. He paused for a few seconds, still holding his cigarette, looked inquiringly at his captive, and then looked away. This time, he took a long puff of his cigarette, held his breath for a second, and slowly blew out smoke in his captive's face.

"I had a business once, you know. I had a good life until your people took it away, just like that. (Pause) Here I'm with nothing, living at my parents'."

"I'm truly sorry about what happened to you. Please let me go," she pleaded.

"I know what's going through your head right now. Do you think my parents will come and save you? Huh?"

His captive didn't say anything but looked at him with tearful eyes that were begging for mercy.

"Do you want to know what happened to my parents, bitch? Huh? They passed away a very long time ago. So nobody will save you!"

"I'm really sorry...please let me go," she cried.

"Let you go? You and I both know that I'm not going to let you go."

"I'm a teacher, not a politician, and I wasn't even..."

"You weren't in Brazzaville during the civil war...blah-blah-blah...I already heard that. Do you think it matters? Huh?" he interjected.

"Please! I'm begging you, please! I'll do anything you want. But please don't kill me," she sobbed.

"I guess you'll have to pay the price for what your people did to me! Take off your clothes, bitch!"

The captive hesitated. Mbingou quickly grabbed his AK47, disengaged the security lock, placed his index finger on the trigger, pointed it at her, and screamed, "Take off your clothes, bitch!" She instinctively raised her hands, trying to protect her face; she trembled, tears streaming down her face, and did as she was ordered. She now tried to cover up her nudity with both hands. Mbingou engaged the security lock and let his AK47 hang from its strap on his back. He grabbed her by the wrists. She made no attempt to resist as he spread her arms open, pinned her against the avocado tree, unzipped his pants, pulled out his manhood, and vigorously thrust it in and out of her a couple of times until he grunted like a pig. He pulled out his manhood, zipped up his pants, took a step back, and sat back down on his bench. He looked content, relaxed, and satisfied. His captive kept eyes on the ground, her hands covering her genitals. She was shaking and sniveling. Mbingou, on the other hand, continued drinking his Ntsamba, used up his packet of cigarettes, pulled some weed out of his back pocket, rolled a blunt, and started puffing on it. He got so high and wasted that he lost control and forgot about his captive. The villagers seized the opportunity, got Mbingou distracted, snuck the captive out of there, and helped her escape.

BOUANSA AND THE AFTERMATH

The victory the rebels achieved in Mouyondzi gave them motivation and boosted their confidence. They looked like a proper army with uniforms, 4x4 vehicles, an endless supply of ammunition, and multiple types of military weapons in their arsenal. They believed they had what it took to frustrate the new administration. They devised a plan of attack, which listed the main villages, towns, and cities they needed to take control of whatever the cost. Bouansa was next on their list. Under the leadership of Kouamoussou, they came with what they believed to be a bulletproof strategy to invade and conquer the town. So in the middle of the night, they took up position on the outskirts of the town and patiently waited until the wee hours of the morning to strike. The government forces were caught by surprise as the rebels engaged them in battle. The town was momentarily enveloped in a cloud of smoke; bullets sparkled like fireworks, leaving behind pools of blood and catastrophe. Assault rifles rattled, grenade and rocket explosions thundered; there were cries and bitter tears everywhere. The train station, where the fighting was the most intense, resembled a dilapidated morgue littered with disjointed dead bodies. The rebels raided the government forces' arsenal and emptied it of its content. They took all the weapons and military equipment away. With the town at their mercy, they helped themselves to the best of everything it could offer. They took money, luxury cars, trucks, fuel, and all other resources they deemed useful to their movement. All in all, they gave a good account of themselves and rose victorious. After two successive victories, they grew in strength, in numbers, and in confidence. They started to believe that they could overthrow Denis Sassou Nguesso's administration.

The rebels drove back to Mouyondzi with their loot, blowing their horns, waving their assault rifles in the air, shouting for joy, dancing in the backs of their vehicles. They received a warm welcome from a group of villagers cheering with broad smiles on their faces, clapping their hands, shouting, "Viva the rebellion!" Children idolized the rebels and a lot more people began to put their faith and trust in them. They started calling them "brave warriors." Day by day, the number of rebels continued to increase as many young people, with their parents' blessings, took interest in the so-called "just cause" and subsequently joined the movement. The new recruits were given quick military training in Nkila-poste and were equipped with an assault rifle, ammunition, a military combat uniform, and assigned to a unit. Mouyondzi developed into the fortress of the rebellion and its capital the breeding ground of warriors. Every time the rebels were not on the battlefield, they enjoyed showing off their driving skills, racing against each other through the dirt roads and dusty streets of the district. Any rebel worthy of the name had to own a car, even if they couldn't drive. They learned how to drive as they stole cars and behaved as if they owned the Earth and all therein. Canteens were opened and a daily flea market was established in the capital. These new canteens had an endless supply of liquor, cigarettes, marijuana, and all sorts of drugs. Most of these places were properties illegally occupied by the rebels, who proudly called themselves "tycoons." The flea market abounded in plundered goods sold at ridiculous prices. Every day wild parties were thrown by the rebels, which usually culminated in mortal gunfights. Sexual immorality, promiscuity, and prostitution prospered, spreading as fast as sexually transmitted diseases.

Days, weeks, and months passed. Mouyondzi wasn't covering itself in glory in the book of the new administration. The iniquities committed by the rebels were weighing heavily on the destiny of my forefathers' land. However, many people from other regions in the south were inspired by the state of anarchy Mouyondzi found itself in and blindly embraced the insidious concept of the rebellion. Like an epidemic, the south of Congo was infected with rebellions that made life a living hell for anybody who decided not to get involved. The rebels, dispersed across the south of the country, began to form alliances with one another. The south was gradually taking the shape of a hell that was poised to break loose at any time.

The rebels were yet to encounter a stumbling block in their dangerous and perennial missions. They were going from victory to victory and from strength to strength. All of their plans of attack progressed as smoothly as they anticipated. They conquered small villages without major problems, invaded train stations in various areas, dismantled large sections of the only railway the country relies on, and succeeded in paralyzing the activities of the Chemin de fer. An economic crisis was slowly suffocating the new administration, as well as the rest of the population who lived in the main cities. This chaotic situation galvanized the rebels, and they felt very close to forcing Denis Sassou Nguesso to negotiate a deal with them.

UNITED FOR THE CAUSE

In a serious turn of events, Mouyondzi as a district decided to stand united in this trying time and grant the rebels full support in their attempt to free Congo from Denis Sassou Nguesso's regime. The traditional leaders of Mouyondzi summoned all sorcerers, wizards, witches, and anybody with extraordinary mystic powers to join the council of sages, who would help to mystically prepare the warriors for their upcoming battles. The meeting took place at the Mbongui in Nkila-poste. Many people came to the meeting. Kingouari, the voice of the movement, addressed the crowd.

"Dear compatriots, we must stand united at this crucial time. The future of our children is at stake. We can no longer sit on the sidelines while the new administration hires mercenaries to violate our rights and kill us in our own country." He paused for a few seconds to gather his thoughts, looked at his audience, who was hanging on to his every word, and added, "We need your help. We're asking those who inherited the powers of our ancestors to join the council of sages."

He paused for almost a full minute. People in the audience looked at each other, murmuring amongst themselves. Kingouari rose up and cleared his throat to get the audience's attention. Everybody went silent and focused their attention back on the speaker. He then continued, "If you know and believe you have what it takes to help advance the movement, we encourage you to join the council. We need your help. Together we can defeat our enemies! It's now or never!"

The audience looked transfixed and couldn't take their eyes off Kingouari, who cleared his throat again.

"On behalf of the movement, we sincerely thank you in advance for your unparalleled support. Dear compatriots, we do thank you for your time and for coming. Viva the rebellion!" He ended his speech shouting the rebellion's new slogan with a raised fist.

A round of applause and cheers erupted from the crowd. A new movement was officially born in which the people of Mouyondzi put their trust, faith, and hope. They didn't approve of the method by which Denis Sassou Nguesso muscled his way back into the presidential seat. Therefore, they rallied behind a movement inspired and led by former army officials and politicians who had served in Pascal Lissouba's administration. Men and women who believed that they had something mystical to offer the movement honored the invitation. These mystics were tasked with anointing the rebels with magical powers so that they might become invincible on the battlefield. Every charlatan, sorcerer, and wizard from all the villages interested in the cause gathered in Nkila-poste. They were working to empower the rebels. Intricate rituals were performed: white roosters were slaughtered, a white sheep was sacrificed, and all forms of dry animal skins and bones and an astounding array of other diverse natural objects were displayed on a red cloth. The booming sound of the African tom-tom filled the air and the ground vibrated as rebels and voodoo masters danced around energetically. They intoned hymns of their ancestors to implore divine guidance. One by one, the rebels were mystically empowered by the council of sages to achieve ineluctable victory. The sages handed the rebels a list of taboos they weren't allowed to break if they wanted to defeat their enemies. While in combat, they were not allowed to pillage, rape, or kill the innocent intentionally. Two days before going to war, they were not allowed to shower, to leave their barracks, or to visit their friends and families.

Their sights were firmly fixed upon Nkayi. Located about

one hundred and fifty kilometers away from Mouyondzi in the south, Nkayi is the fourth-largest city in Congo. The city boasts the largest sugar cane plantation and the only sugar factory in the entire country. The government forces had the city well guarded to the best of their knowledge. But the rebels knew the city better than their enemies, since the majority of them had at some point lived, traded, or often visited the city on a regular basis. Endowed by the sages of Mouyondzi with the mystical powers of their ancestors, the rebels felt invincible and were primed and eager to attack and conquer Nkayi. They quietly encircled the city late in the afternoon and patiently waited for nightfall to commence their suicide mission.

As planned, the rebels launched a well-planned attack on Nkayi in the still of the night. The government forces were caught by surprise. They had anticipated a monstrous attack at some point, but not as early as this. Both camps did not hesitate to use their armaments on each other. It was do or die. I got so used to hearing the sounds of machine guns that I could easily distinguish the weapon by its sound. From the hills of Nkenge, we could still hear the terrifying sounds of 127s, mortars, assault rifles, tanks, and rockets rattle, rumble, thunder, and boom. Every now and then we could feel the Earth vibrate gently beneath our feet as heavy army machinery spat out explosions. The rebels valiantly rose victorious after forty-eight hours of intense combat. Many soldiers from the losing side took refuge in the massive sugar cane plantation. The city finally fell under the rebels' control, who couldn't resist the sweet temptation of pillaging it. Every place of commerce was scanned for money and robbed. During their fleeting occupation of the city, a disagreement occurred amongst the rebels about who would assume the position of governor of the city in the interim. They eventually agreed to offer Kouamoussou, one of the leaders, the position.

While the rebels were distracted by their victory and the ineffable joy of satisfying their selfish interests in Nkayi, their enemies were regrouping and reorganizing themselves, receiving backup from Pointe-Noire, Loubomo, and Brazzaville in the form of manpower, weapons, ammunition, and logistical support. The rebels passionately invested time and energy into looting and transporting their newly-acquired treasures to Mouyondzi, their fortress. For a few weeks, they naïvely believed they had defeated their foes to the point of no recovery. But their victory was short-lived. They underestimated their enemies and did not take them seriously.

This time, the government forces were better prepared and equipped and came back when the rebels least expected them. They tried to put up a fight, but they weren't evenly matched this time. The tables were turned and the rebels were to receive a taste of their own medicine. The government forces successfully conquered the city once again, reinforced security, and turned it into a military base. From there, they could strategize to find a way to crush and nullify the rebellion that was plaguing the south of the country.

Now that the rebels had stared defeat in the face, their zeal to continue waging war against the government forces was slowly dwindling away. They exited Nkayi at a blistering pace, their tails between their legs, and convincingly defeated. The rebels suffered a huge setback in their original ambition, and they could no longer move forward because they lacked self-discipline, their logistical support dismally failed them, and their enemies grew stronger than ever. So the rebels were restricted to assuring the protection of Bouansa and Mouyondzi against an impending attack from their sworn enemies. Since they still had control of the country's main power plant, they took pleasure in depriving bigger cities of electricity whenever they felt like it. On a few occasions, they threatened to dismantle and destroy it entirely if their enemies dared fight their way into Mouyondzi. In response to this threat, the president swore to slaughter everything that moved in Mouyondzi if the rebels destroyed Congo's only main electricity source. Days of anarchy crowned with political uncertainty stretched longer than we could have all imagined.

Kouamoussou, the self-proclaimed general, spread a rumor that they had managed to establish contact with the former leaders of the country, who were in exile abroad. These political leaders had apparently vowed to support the movement and had promised to supply military weapons and equipment to the rebels until they deposed Denis Sassou Nguesso's administration. Therefore, the rebels were asked to wait for army helicopters to drop off supplies on the rice field in Songamerica (Nkila-poste).

The population congregated at the Mbongui, where Kingouari addressed the audience. He looked a little tired but sounded defiant and confident in his speech. He said, "We have fought our enemies with limited resources. In the face of strong opposition, we neither faltered nor backed down. We're brave and mighty warriors determined to win. Our intrepidity is second to none!" He paused for a few seconds as he always did. The audience was silent and attentive. He then continued with the same zest as before, "Our movement has caught the attention of the former leaders of this country in exile abroad. According to our reliable sources, they have pledged to supply us with armaments and the logistical support we need in order to topple the new administration. (Pause) We're saying no to dictatorship! Viva the rebellion!"

This rumor injected a sense of renewed hope in the waning rebellion. The rebels got over-excited and spread the good news across Mouyondzi. In vain, the rebels waited for the helicopters to bring the supplies they desperately needed. Every night they would make a huge fire, congregate around it, and wait for the helicopters that never showed up. However, the rebels' strong belief in those political leaders encouraged them to wait faithfully. Slowly but surely the place turned into a camping site. Like pilgrims in the Promised Land, they prayed and believed that their needs would be met. Every time they heard the noise of an aircraft flying across the sky, they would brandish burning wood, and shout, "Over here! Over here!" They had placed their hope, faith, and trust in a barren promise rooted in a rumor. They were becoming unhinged.

CHRISTMAS AND NEW YEAR

Every Christmas Eve, my friends and I would go to the Saint Jean Bosco Cathedral in Fond Tié-Tié. The cathedral would be teeming with people. The play, celebrations, Mass, and the atmosphere were always amazing. Everybody looked cheerful and radiated positive energy. That was the atmosphere I always wished to see for everybody across the world; that was the world I wanted to live in. I always looked forward to that day. December 24, 1998, I felt depressed. I closed my eyes, trying to fall asleep, but to no avail. There was a curfew and in the distance, I could hear assault rifles rattling away. The clock ticked away; somehow my body managed to relax, and I drifted off to sleep.

On December 25, 1998 I sat on my bed in the guest room at Papa Ndazet's house. I felt nostalgic. I remembered how much I used to like the smell of new plastic toys; I would get excited to wear my new clothes and shoes. My friends and I would get together, walk around the neighborhood, show off our new outfits and toys, and play for hours.

"Everything is subject to change. This is just a season and it's temporary," I mumbled.

The feeling of doom and gloom weighed heavily on my emotions. I struggled to blink back the tears as I remembered what my father always used to say to me: "Men aren't supposed to cry. Crying is a sign of weakness." So I looked at the ceiling and blinked back my tears. For the first time in my life, Christmas Day was devoid of any Christmas spirit. Father Christmas didn't drop by for the children. The rebellion deprived the people of their

Christmas miracle. New Year's Eve and New Year's Day passed by unnoticed. There was no celebration during the entire festive season. Many times I closed my eyes, quieted my mind, focused, and tried to dream and picture myself in a peaceful and perfect world, a world where everybody loved each other unconditionally, had empathy and sympathy for their neighbor, a world where nobody had to suffer injustice, and where everybody was free and enjoyed themselves. I always wished I could miraculously find myself in that perfect world once I'd opened my eyes. But each time reality proved to me otherwise. I found myself trapped in a place where injustice, hate, persecution, and evil in its multiple forms were rampant.

THE NOUVEAU RICHE, BONZA BORE

The rebellion continued spawning interesting characters. New young millionaires emerged after robbing banks, stores, and companies during the brief occupation of Nkayi. There were tons of easy cash in the hands of individuals who didn't sweat for it. They enjoyed showing off their newly acquired riches. They threw money at every problem. Guns, money, drugs, alcohol, and whores dictated their new lifestyles. One of those interesting characters went by the alias Bonza Bore, the nouveau riche. Nobody really knew what his real name was. He was in his early twenties, skinny, and stood about six feet tall. He decided to leave the rebellion after the victory they'd achieved in Nkayi. He singlehandedly pillaged over thirty-six million francs CFA from the bank and lost his left arm in a grenade explosion. "I'm rich beyond my wildest dreams, and I'm on top of the world," he would often boast.

Money went to his head. He hired twenty bodyguards whom he equipped with five cars, guns, and military uniforms. He took over a sumptuous house, which used to belong to some politician in exile, and made it his castle. He had money and power, but was still missing a woman in his life. Therefore, he took off on a quest for love across Mouyondzi. The king met an attractive woman, a whore, who he married on the same day. He was over the moon, but his happiness was short-lived.

A few weeks into the matrimony, Bonza Bore caught his wife in bed with another warrior. He tortured and savagely killed them both and ordered his bodyguards to dispose of the bodies in plain sight. The incident earned Bonza Bore notoriety across the district. His reputation preceded him everywhere he went. He chose to never pay for anything, used violence and brutality to get whatever he wanted, and became the local farmers' worst nightmare. He and his henchmen went hunting for sport on private farms. Farmers who dared stop them didn't live to tell the tale. They continued living a life of crime. One day he got into a silly argument about girls with two brothers at a local bar in Mpanga. Bonza Bore didn't hesitate to kill them both and ran away with his henchmen. The villagers got furious and went on a witch-hunt. But their targets moved to another village, altered their routine, and were nowhere to be found.

EN ROUTE TO NKENGE

Days went by, and the possibility of a sudden invasion by the government forces looked more and more imminent. They forced their way through Bouansa, purged the place of rebels, and set up checkpoints everywhere to secure it. The rebels were pushed back to the bridge of Niari, which is the border separating Bouansa from Mouyondzi. They were no longer in a position to attack the government forces so they went on the defensive. They reinforced security and stood guard day and night at the Niari Bridge to prevent their enemies from flooding into Mouyondzi.

Papa Ndazet grew increasingly worried and could no longer bear the thought of me being around. He ordered me to go and stay with my mother in Nkenge, ten kilometers west of Nkila-poste.

"You have to go and stay at your mother's at once, son!"

He looked stressed and restless as he paced back and forth in his dining room like a caged animal. His voice sounded a little shaky, which was unlike him. I was sitting at the table across from where he was. I empathized with him because times were hard for everybody. I looked downcast and my brain was frazzled. I didn't know what to say, although I understood him. I had my hands on the table, twiddling with a black thread I'd picked up from the floor earlier. I remained silent.

"Nkila-poste is no longer safe for anybody right now. Do you understand what I'm saying, son?"

"Yes father, I understand," I replied in such a low voice that my response sounded more like a whisper.

"You're always welcome here, and you know that. But this is not the right time," he explained.

"Yes Papa Ndazet, I understand," I blurted.

"But at this present time, it is safer in Nkenge at your mother's than it is here with me," he stressed.

"What about the fabrics?" I asked.

"Don't worry about it. I'll handle it, son. And if the ancestors protect and help us survive this volatile situation, I'll make sure that you get your money. Right now, the main priority is to try to remain alive somehow," he assured me.

I trusted Papa Ndazet completely. He was always true to his word. He never made promises he could not keep. I felt relieved that Papa Ndazet promised to help me with my merchandise. I had no time to waste. I packed what I needed and hit the road. I set out for a long walk to my mother's village, Nkenge. I had done this walk a few times before, and enjoyed it each time. I quite like walking in nature. During this time of political uncertainty I intentionally took time to really enjoy it, to breathe the fresh air, to marvel at the trees, shrubs, flowers, streams, insects, birds, hills, mountains, plains, and to bask in nature's enchanting beauty. I thought to myself, *This could be the last time I walk this road.* I arrived in Nkenge in the evening and heaved a sigh of relief when I saw my mother and youngest sister Leolin, whom I hadn't seen in two years. I was delighted that they were alive and well. Upon seeing my family, all of my worries disappeared for a minute, and my heart was filled with joy.

AT MY MOTHER'S

"Look at you, all grown up!" my mother excitedly exclaimed, her eyes gleaming with joy.

She hugged me and kept me in her embrace for almost a minute. I felt tears trickle down my neck. She couldn't contain her emotions. She was very happy to see her only son. But, considering the volatile situation Mouyondzi found itself in, the timing for my trip there was totally off. She couldn't hide her frustration or mince her words about it. She was furious with my father.

"Why did your foolish father send you here? What's wrong with him? Of all places, why this godforsaken place?" she stormed.

"Can I at least put my bag down, Mum?" I asked sounding a little annoyed.

She ignored my question and shook her head in frustration. She put her hands on her waist, was standing with her legs spraddled in her front yard, looking through me, with a mutter of disgust, shrugging her shoulders. I was familiar with that stance, which brought back memories of my mother arguing with my father. I finally put my bag down, and my little sister Leolin came running toward me with her arms open wide. I picked her up and hugged her affectionately. She wrapped her arms around me and rested her head on my shoulder. She soon fell asleep in my arms as we went from door to door to greet my grandparents, uncles, cousins, aunts, nieces, and nephews. A loving mother is an endless source of ineffable joy, peace, comfort, and all the wonderful emotions words cannot express. Being around my mother made me feel at ease. I felt very happy, like my normal self again. The night looked magical: a billion stars sparkled across the wide face of the sky, fireflies twinkled on the grass, crickets were chirping, cicadas buzzing, dogs barking, and owls ululating, and I was feeling particularly fantastic. My mother and I sat around the fire burning gracefully in the middle of her brick house and conversed while Leolin was fast asleep.

"Did you have a safe trip, son?" she asked.

"Yes, I did. Thanks," I replied.

"How are the soldiers treating passengers on the train?" she inquired.

"You don't want to know. It's like hell in a cell," I revealed.

"Is it that bad?" she asked, sounding surprised.

"Yes indeed, it is. Nowadays a journey by train is an adventure I wouldn't recommend to anyone," I said.

She kept quiet for a second, looked at me inquiringly, scratched and shook her head in disbelief, and asked in a voice filled with frustration, "Why did you agree to make the trip now?"

Here we go again, I thought to myself. I sensed all along that she was looking for an opening to give me grief about the whole situation. So I kept my eyes on the fire burning gracefully and sighed, "I had no idea how bad things were until I boarded the train."

"Don't you follow the news?"

"No, I don't. I have been trying to stay away from anything negative. And the news does nothing but report everything negative," I said.

My mother looked at me with pity in her eyes, continued shaking her head in disbelief, smiled a little, lowered her voice to a whisper, and confided, "The new administration has been planning on arresting politicians, army officials, and soldiers who served under and fought for Pascal Lissouba during the civil war. And there are many of them dispersed across Mouyondzi."

"I don't know what else to say, Mum. I'm already here and

cannot return to Pointe-Noire now, even if I desperately want to," I said.

"Well, I guess we'll have to find a way to survive."

My mother and I sat in silence for a while. She added more wood to the waning fire, which crackled and fizzled as the flame got bigger, and it felt soothing and relaxing. I tried to steer the conversation toward my upcoming trip to Brazzaville.

"Hey! I'll be going to university in Brazzaville soon, Mum," I said with a smile on my face.

"Congratulations, son! I was very happy when I got the news! You made me very proud!" she exclaimed, her face gleaming with a smile.

I felt so good and honored that I could put a smile on my parents' faces. I was determined to achieve more success in life, so that I could create more amazing memories to enjoy with my parents.

"Dad is short of money to finance my university studies at the moment. That's the main reason why I'm here—to sell some fabrics. The plan is to raise enough funds for university," I explained.

"Huh? That's absolute nonsense!" my mother said, dismissing my explanation.

"Why is that, Mum?" I wailed.

I wasn't particularly curious to find out her take on my father's plan because I already knew how she felt. She stood up, threw her hands in the air in frustration, shrugged her shoulders, and said, "I know your father better than you do, son. I was married to him for many years. Your father can't fool me! He has enough money to send you to university, trust me, son. If you were one of his nephews or nieces, the story would have been different. He always has more than enough money for his brothers, sisters, nephews, and nieces."

"Mum, the last thing I want is to argue with you. I know that you and Dad have your differences, but…"

I did not have a chance to finish my sentence before my

mother interrupted me. She was such a feisty woman and quick-tempered. And any topic that involved my father got her riled up, which led me to believe that the divorce left a sour taste in her mouth.

"The man has not changed; he keeps doing the same thing over and over again."

"Is there anything else he did I'm not aware of?"

"He happily and freely spends money on supporting his nieces, nephews, brothers, sisters, cousins, mistresses, and everybody else. He's always put other people's needs before those of his own children."

"Maybe those people were in serious need of help, Mum."

"All those bloody people he keeps giving money to are neither poor nor destitute. He's always trying to save the world while letting his own family down."

"Mum, I believe there's a good reason for it."

"A good reason, huh? Why do you think your father and I argued constantly?" she stormed.

"You're my mother, and he is my father. As your son, I can't take sides. I'll always love you both unconditionally," I replied.

"Your father's decision to send you here now was both careless and irresponsible. He shouldn't have sent you here now! If anything happens to you, I'll kill him with my bare hands!" she snapped.

"Dad meant well, Mum. I don't believe he was trying to put me in harm's way."

"Are you even listening to yourself?"

"If he knew how volatile the situation was, he wouldn't have sent me here. I do agree with you that the man has his flaws. But who doesn't?" I said in my dad's defense.

"You think that your father is a saint, don't you? This is irresponsible and unacceptable!" she stormed.

"I didn't say he was a saint. Dad has my best interests at heart. He wouldn't knowingly send me to a place that was likely to become a human butchery."

"You obviously don't know your father better than I do, do you?"

"Mum, what loving father in this world would do something like that? The idea behind the whole trip was to kill two birds with one stone."

"Kill two birds with one stone? Huh? We're the only birds that are likely to get killed."

"Mum, I hadn't seen you in two years. Dad thought a trip here to visit you would be good and also help me make some money for Brazzaville," I said.

"You and I wouldn't be having this conversation if Mouyondzi did not find itself in such a volatile situation. And yes, your father has your best interests at heart. But I'm still very angry with him. I think your father likes making me angry."

After a long and heated conversation with my mother, I surmised that I couldn't change her mind. She had a set opinion about my dad and it wasn't positive. I also sensed that my parents still had outstanding issues that they didn't fully address when they got divorced. I kept quiet and this time there was an awkward silence between us. I knew my mother was still fuming inside. She was the type of person who would never let go easily. She sat back down, stoked the fire, put her right hand on her cheek, and rested her elbow in the palm of her left hand. We were both staring at the fire in silence. Once again, I tried to change the conversation.

"What's new around here, Mum?"

"Nothing new apart from the impending invasion of the government forces," she replied in a sad voice.

"Is that so? Isn't it just a rumor?"

"I wish it were, son. The information comes from reliable sources. Unfortunately for us, it is likely to happen sooner than we think," she said.

"I don't know what to think anymore. Everybody has been saying something different."

"Don't be fooled, son! Government forces are threatening to

avenge their comrades who were beaten before being brutally killed here," she whispered.

My brain was frazzled, and I was getting fed up with all the rumors. *Whatever happens happens! I'll cross that bridge when I get there,* I thought.

"Nobody in the district will be safe; no life will be spared. Most soldiers that compose the government forces are former Rwandese rebels and Angolan soldiers who are trained killers," she whispered.

"I'm already here, Mum. There is absolutely nothing anybody can do to reverse what is happening right now."

"It is easy for you to say, isn't it?" she asked, quickly shoving a twig into the fire.

I knew she wasn't done yet. She was still trying to drum the reality into my head until I admitted how reckless and irresponsible my father's plan was. But I wisely refused to be drawn into that game.

"Mum, right now all we can do is wait and see what happens. Nothing can turn back the clock," I ended.

My mother and I eventually changed the conversation, laughed, and reminisced. The beautiful bonfire was still burning gracefully. Through the ajar door, I could see the glorious moonlight bathing the land of my ancestors. The house felt warm, cozy, and the atmosphere relaxing. I was very happy to be in my mother's presence again. Memories of my childhood replayed in my mind. I remember how she used to treat me like a prince. She was very protective of me since I was her only son. My mother's love was both a source of ineffable joy to me and deeply therapeutic. We talked for hours, catching up, until I drifted off to sleep. The sound of AK47s continued to rattle in the distance throughout the night but I didn't wake up even once.

Early in the morning my mother had already gone to her farm to collect some fruits, mushrooms, and vegetables for breakfast. Leolin was still sleeping. I was sitting on a stool by the door, watching and enjoying the sunrise, when one of my favorite uncles named Mwini came for a visit. He gave me a big and warm hug, welcomed me to Nkenge, went quickly inside the house to grab another stool, and sat beside me.

"When did you get here?" he inquired.

"I got here last night. We tried dropping by your place but you weren't there," I explained.

"Oh! Sorry! I was out and about, running some errands in Mouandi," he said.

I gave Noko Mwini all the news he needed to know about the rest of the family in Pointe-Noire and shared with him the reason I found myself in Mouyondzi now, not in Brazzaville. To my surprise, he didn't lecture about how unwise and reckless my father's plan was.

"It's a pity that there's so much confusion in the country right now," he said.

"Yes indeed. Sadly, that seems to be the prevailing reality at the moment," I echoed his statement.

"Control and power are the root cause of the ongoing struggle between the rebels and the new administration," he explained.

"I still don't get it. What does it take for people to live in peace and harmony? Aren't we all foreigners on this Earth?" I thought out loud.

"Sadly, we live in a country where it seems that the strong continuously devour the weak," he pointed out.

"I have absolutely no idea where this country is heading. All these senseless killings and constant persecution of civilians make me wonder if there is ever going to be light at the end of the tunnel," I wondered.

"Light at the end of the tunnel? I highly doubt it because people seem to be obsessed with power and control so they can do as they please and take ownership of the country's natural resources."

"They must be delusional to think that way because everybody comes into this world with nothing and returns to the bosom of the Earth with nothing," I said.

"That's right, my nephew! You and I understand that. But try explaining it both to the new administration and to all these rebels."

"I can't stand these rebels! Their recklessness has put us all in danger."

"Do not worry! Justice will be done. They'll never go unpunished for their crimes," he confidently said.

"I hope so, Noko Mwini. In this country, the wicked seem to get away with wrongdoing."

"Justice will be done. And things will work out for the best, you'll see. Just wait and see."

"You sound so optimistic, Noko Mwini."

"In times like these, people can choose to either stay optimistic or pessimistic. And I'm one of those people who chooses to stay optimistic."

Positive energy and positive thinking were exactly what I needed. I felt a sense of security around my maternal family. Their unconditional love felt like a shield of protection to me. Talking to Noko Mwini was refreshing. In hindsight, I was grateful to Papa Ndazet for urging me to come to Nkenge.

SADNESS AND JOY

Shortly after I had arrived in Nkenge, my grandfather fell seriously ill. He was in his late seventies, looked weak, and was very tired all the time. The current volatile situation across Mouyondzi made it extremely difficult to take him to any hospital for treatment. The main hospital in Mouyondzi is located in Nkila-poste. My grandfather refused to be taken there and resigned himself to the thought of dying quietly and peacefully in his hut. His health was deteriorating fast. Before passing away, he had a chance to address his family.

"I'm ready to travel to the land of my ancestors," he confided.

My grandfather paused for a minute, coughed, and asked for a glass of water. He was in pain, his breath was coming in gasps, and he was struggling to speak. But he was determined to say a few words to his family for the last time.

"I have been blessed with healthy children, grandchildren, and great-grandchildren."

He paused, trying to summon every bit of his remaining strength. His voice sounded feeble as he managed to whisper, "I'm grateful to the ancestors for everything. My last prayer is for the ancestors to watch over every member of my family and to protect each one of you."

We all watched helplessly as my grandfather exhaled his last breath. He looked peaceful. My grandfather was no more. He had traveled to the land of his ancestors. There was silence in the room for a minute, followed by cries and tears. Personally, I envied his peaceful death in the presence of his spouse, children, grandchildren, and great-grandchildren. If I were to choose how I would want to exit this world, I would be happy to go out in the same way as my grandfather. At that particular moment, I honestly wished I could have traded places with him, because I wasn't looking forward to being hunted down in the jungles of Mouyondzi like a wild animal for the rebellion I didn't support or perpetrate. I was sick and tired of the ongoing struggle. I desperately needed some rest. My grandfather was a member of the local Protestant church in Nkenge. So the congregation took charge of the funeral. His coffin was lowered into the sacred ground beside the graves of his late relatives. After my grandfather's death, my grandmother constantly prayed to God with diligence to take her life away. There was a lot of doom and gloom around. Everybody looked sad, worried, afraid, despondent, and restless.

The whole gloomy atmosphere inspired Noko Moussoki to come up with a brilliant idea. I was visiting at my grandmother's when he told me about it. He was trying to bring some joy back to the villagers.

"Even in a time so gloomy as this, we can still live life with joy."

I stopped playing and joking around with my cousins and focused my attention on him.

"What do you mean?" I inquired.

He was sitting on a wooden chair positioned against the wall by the small window overlooking the forest main path, stroking his moustache with his right hand while his left hand rested on the table. He looked pensive and sounded inspired.

"Joy must come from within, not from external circumstances," he said.

"Look around, Noko Moussoki! There's nothing but crying and tears."

"This world is full of crying and tears every day, I know. Right now, somewhere in this world, there are people who are going through situations far worse than ours. Do we wallow in self-pity and sadness? Or do we find ways to keep our heads up?"

He was making some valid points, which made me examine my whole attitude and approach to the circumstances we found ourselves in.

"You may be right in theory, but I don't know what to think right now," I replied.

"My nephew, you can't choose your reality, but you can choose your attitude. So you can choose to stay positive or negative. Your circumstances cannot choose your attitude, but you definitely can," he explained.

"I don't know, Noko Moussoki," I said.

"We shouldn't let temporary difficult circumstances take away our ability to live life to the fullest. We're always free to choose our attitude, remember that."

"In trying times such as these, like most here, I'm honestly struggling to think positively and keep my head up."

"Hear me out, nephew. I have an idea about what we can do to help lift the morale in this village."

"Huh? Tell me more, please. You now have my undivided attention!" I exclaimed sounding both surprised and intrigued. I grabbed a stool, sat beside him, and hung on to every word.

"I have been toying with the idea of assembling a group of four or five young men like yourself to start a band. I think some music will help make people around here feel a little better. Don't you think?" he smiled.

His idea changed my mood, got me curious, and I wanted to find out more details about it.

"Huh? You want to start a band in the middle of this mess?"

"Yes, I certainly do! Through music we can tune out the sadness, worries, fear, restlessness, or any form of negativity trying to bring us down. And we can definitely experience the joy within that gives us hope for a brighter future," he said.

"Wow, Noko Moussoki. This sounds like an amazing idea. I want to be a part of it," I enthused, now convinced of the merit of his idea.

"Very good. Here is what we're going to do: find other guys

interested in the idea and have them meet with me later this evening so we can get started."

I talked to Jules and Ngoma about my uncle's idea. Jules and Ngoma were two nice young fellows from Nkenge who I had grown to like and become friends with. They were very interested in the idea and were thrilled to join. We got together and started a band called Super Accent. Noko Moussoki had been a musician for a long time. He started coaching and giving us singing lessons. He had a big repertoire of songs that he'd composed and performed many times and he taught us some of those songs. Every night under the moonlight and a myriad of stars, we would gather in front of Mwini's restaurant to rehearse the songs, perform for a small audience, and have a good time. We always looked forward to rehearsing every night after long days of working hard with our parents on the farms. Music proved to be an effective escape. In music, we all had something positive to look forward to and through music we could forget our problems for a while. We could imagine a world of absolute peace and love that superseded the misery we had to endure in a physical world full of injustice. We would sing the nights away, put smiles on sad faces, and enjoy ourselves despite our circumstances.

THE RACE FOR SURVIVAL

Violence intensified across Mouyondzi and perverted people with twisted minds grew ingenious in their immorality. Needless to say, individuals like Bonza Bore and his gang were still making waves across the district. People from many villages where he and his henchmen had caused so much heartache organized themselves and decided to take matters into their own hands. Bonza Bore and his gang were wanted. So they made themselves scarce and would operate mostly at night. They were still unrepentant and continued with the same lifestyle. His reputation preceded him wherever he and his gang went. Over time, his resources were depleting fast and his influence waning. The district became too small a place for him and his henchmen to hide. One day while they were trying to sneak their way out of the district, the villagers managed to catch them and brought them back to Nkila-poste. They disarmed, undressed, and tied them up in the center of the soccer field. Before giving them a taste of their own medicine, they were interrogated by the villagers.

"You, the ring leader, alias Bonza Bore, why did you kill the Tongo brothers? Do you have any idea how much pain and suffering you inflicted on the Tongo family and the whole village?"

"The Tongo brothers crossed me and they deserved to die! I feel no remorse for killing them!" he scoffed.

The villagers were emotionally charged. They couldn't contain their rage. They slapped Bonza Bore and his henchmen across their faces with the flat side of their machetes. They twisted around in pain.

"You live by the sword you die by the sword! You know what that means, huh? Huh?" they shouted.

Bonza Bore and his bodyguards remained silent and looked unrepentant in the face of the cavalry. They knew that the time had arrived for them to reap the consequences of the seeds of violence they'd been sowing everywhere they went.

"Bring the tires and gasoline and let's set these useless bastards ablaze!" villagers angrily ordered.

Twenty worn-out tires were wheeled to the center of the field, along with a twenty-five liter drum of gasoline. Each of the killers wore a tire around their waist, which were set on fire. Bonza Bore and his bodyguards screamed in agony as their flesh and hair burnt in the flames of hell. Their eyes and bellies burst open in the blaze. Many minutes passed, and Bonza Bore and his bodyguards were reduced to nothing but a heap of ashes. The chapter of their pathetic existence was finally closed and faded into oblivion for eternity.

Meanwhile, the forces of the government continued fighting the rebels at the Niari Bridge. They had been trying to force their way into Mouyondzi in order to deal a final and fatal blow to the heart of the rebellion. The fighting intensified; the rebellion progressively faltered, weakened, and shrank to a hopeless resistance. Things weren't looking good for the rebels. They summoned every bit of strength left in them to try and stand tall in the face of mounting pressure and adversity. They desperately continued to fight tooth and nail as they tried to hold onto the land of milk and honey of their own creation. The enemies' tanks and heavy artillery spat out multiple explosions, followed by a rain of bullets, causing the rebels to retreat and run for cover. The attacks escalated; the rebels could no longer continue fighting, nor could they stop government forces from swarming into the district like a hive of irritated bees. There were a lot of casualties in the rebels' camp. Kimpoungou and Ntsende perished on the battlefield. Mbingou survived by the skin of his teeth and fled to Kingoué. Kouamoussou escaped and was rumored to have made it safely overseas. Like an incurable epidemic, the enemies quickly spread across Mouyondzi. The hedge of protection erected by the rebels at the Niari Bridge was violently blasted open. The predators that we all dreaded were officially in the vicinity and they were on the prowl.

The sacred land of our ancestors was stained with blood. Like the sound of several thunderstorms, the enemies' heavy artillery rumbled, rattled, blasted, boomed, and echoed across the whole district.

"Run for your lives! As fast as you can, run!" somebody screamed.

"The enemies are getting closer! Let's all get the hell out of here!" another person shouted.

"Drop everything, just get away quickly!" somebody else shouted.

"My kids, where are my kids?" a mother cried.

"Lord, have mercy!" somebody else whispered.

The enemies marched valiantly and triumphantly through villages, setting huts and houses on fire and gunning down people who were slow to seek cover or those who wasted valuable time trying to hide their belongings. People with physical disabilities who could not escape were killed. After the sudden invasion of our enemies, we all instinctively dropped to the ground and cautiously slithered our way into the forests close to our homes. From far away one could hear the sound of the enemies' footsteps; one could see dust rise into the sky as they marched triumphantly through the main dirt road in our village. They shot at anything, at any living form that moved or made a sound. They were marking their territory, sending a strong message to everybody that they had finally arrived and were officially in control of the whole district. They went directly to the country's main power plant in Moukoukoulou, which is not far away from Nkenge. They caught the few rebels by surprise who had been tasked with guarding the plant. Some escaped by the skin of their teeth, while others were held captive and savagely killed a few days later, after being rigorously interrogated.

Like everybody else, Noko Mwini, my mother, Leolin, and I took off running as a group and found refuge in the dense forest of Nkenge called Boussaka. The forest belongs to my grandparents, so my mother and Noko Mwini knew how to navigate their way through. With our bare hands, we cleared a small section of the Boussaka and collected dry and straight branches, strong vines, and banana and palm leaves to build a shelter. We all got to work and within an hour, the shelter was standing. We had a rectangular roof covered in banana and palm leaves, and strong vines were used as ropes to hold the structure together. We all sat on the thin mattress Noko Mwini managed to grab when we escaped. Everybody was confused about what was happening. Nobody knew anything about the whereabouts of the enemies. We had no clue how long we were going to have to stay hidden in the forest. Heavy rain bucketed through our shelter. We got drenched to our bones. Huddled together like a pack of squirrel monkeys in the Amazon, we trembled with cold throughout the night. For safety reasons, we had to whisper or use made-up sign language when communicating with each other. Any loud noises would easily lead enemies to our hiding spot. The fear of being captured or dying brutally at the hands of our enemies kept me awake. I couldn't sleep, no matter how hard I tried. I could not see my uncle, mother, and sister sleeping next to me: it was literally the darkest night of my life. The night dragged on for eternity; it felt like a billion years. I had to wait patiently for morning to figure out how to survive in the wild for who knows how long. It looked as though we were all playing a waiting game. So, on the edge of the mattress, I silently waited once more. Due to the complexity of the situation, I truly didn't know what I was waiting for. I could hear Noko Mwini stand up and walk a few meters away from the shelter to use the toilet. His sight was sharp in the dark. He paced carefully back to the shelter and sat beside me.

"What a night!" he exclaimed.

"An eventful night, indeed!" I replied, shaking my head in disbelief.

"It's unfortunate and revolting that we the innocent always end up getting caught in the middle of the senseless power struggle," he complained.

"Now the rebels are nowhere to be found. They have vanished into thin air. Unfortunately, the innocent have to pay the price for the blunders of a rebellion they didn't perpetrate," I angrily said.

"Sadly, that's the brutal truth and it's a bitter pill to swallow."

"What frustrates me even more is the fact that the government forces assume we were all rebels or affiliated with the rebellion somehow," I said, sounding very annoyed.

"We can only hope and pray that nothing horrible happens to us, because the government forces are certainly not here on a humanitarian mission," he said worriedly.

I was rocking back and forth where I sat in a fetal position. I could barely see Noko Mwini in the obscurity, but I could hear him cracking twigs with his fingers. We both fell silent for a minute. The forest was quiet; even wild animals did not make a sound, but every now and then the trademark rattling noise of AK47s could be heard in the distance. I was beginning to zone out when Noko Mwini said, "Tomorrow night, I'm going to sneak back into the village to retrieve utensils and other useful tools we need during our time in the wild. I can't live in the wild with nothing to work with."

"Don't you think it is still risky to sneak back into the village so soon?" I asked him.

"I'll be in and out in a matter of seconds," Noko Mwini said.

"I still think that we should wait until we have information about the whereabouts of the government forces," I tried to reason with him.

"The fact is we're already in tremendous danger. They could be anywhere for all we know, and this is not a fortress! We can't let irrational fear dictate every move we try to make," he said, sounding a little annoyed by my protest.

"Can't we live without utensils for a few days? We're hiding from trained killers who wouldn't hesitate to gun down anybody. I strongly suggest that we wait here a little longer for our own safety. Don't you agree?" I pleaded

"In times like these, one needs to be brave. Death comes for all of us sooner or later. Don't worry, nephew! I'll be just fine."

I eventually came to the conclusion that I was wasting my time because Noko Mwini was adamant about making a quick trip back to the village. So I gave up trying to convince him otherwise. Our conversation ended up waking my mother, who then joined us and started to whine about our precarious situation.

"Who is going to protect or save us now? The new administration has sent its troops here to hunt us down. But why?" my mother said.

"Don't worry, Mum! The new administration will face the international community if its troops dare to wipe all of us out. That will be genocide!" I explained.

"Don't be naïve, nephew! The international community doesn't even know we exist, let alone listen to our plight. Did the international community intervene to stop the senseless killing during the civil war in Brazzaville?" Noko Mwini asked.

I had nothing to say to that because I couldn't argue with facts.

"Huh? My point exactly! Forget the international community! We have to rely on ourselves and find a way to survive," he stressed.

"They'll soon be alerted of this injustice," I said.

"The new administration controls the media in this country. Do you think the media will report exactly what's happening right now? I highly doubt it! The media is biased toward the government. There is no freedom of press. The truth is swept under the rug and the innocent like you and I continue to suffer injustice."

We talked for hours about our current situation, the media, the new administration, the international community, and the United Nations. Noko Mwini made some valid points.

The truth is often swept under the rug. One cannot count on the biased media to report the truth. The new administration is in control of the media. It's an uphill battle for the innocent, who continue paying the price. The only hope for survival for us was to trust the Divine and earnestly pray for a miracle.

THE REST OF THE FAMILY

The surprise arrival of the government troops in the district forced everybody to disperse and seek refuge in the forests. In the panic, chaos, rush, and confusion families were separated; they took off running without looking back. At the break of dawn, Noko Mwini and I set out to find where my grandmother and the rest of our family members went to hide. My mother offered to tag along, but we wouldn't let her come with us. She worried about everybody and wanted to protect me somehow.

"Be careful, my son! Mwini, do look after him! Don't let him out of your sight, please…" my mother said worriedly.

"Don't worry, sister, we'll be all right. Nothing will befall us! The spirits of the ancestors are with us. They'll guide us every step of the way. We shall return here in one piece, not in pieces," he chuckled.

Despite the injustice we were forced to suffer, my Uncle Mwini didn't lose his sense of humor. He was courageous, intelligent, wise, and funny. I enjoyed talking to him, because he always seemed to know exactly what to say to give me hope whenever I felt doomed to perish at the hands of the government forces. I drew a lot of spiritual strength from him, which kept me going during those dark days.

"I'll be fine, Mum. We'll be back as quickly as we can," I reassured her.

My mother hugged me affectionately, looked me in the eye, and reluctantly released me from her embrace. At no time did she want me to leave our hiding spot. I knew how much it broke her heart to see me leave. But I couldn't help it; our survival in those times of trouble required that we take calculated risks and a bit of intrepidity. There was no time to play Mummy's boy. I saw tears of inquietude drown her piercing brown eyes. For a second, I was transfixed, as if daydreaming, and felt sadness wash over me as I looked into her tearful eyes. I shrugged my shoulders apologetically, turned away, and followed Noko Mwini.

"Let's go! Follow me this way!"

We walked through thick bushes toward the section of the forest where Noko Mwini guessed the rest of our family members would be. I followed Noko Mwini carefully as he paced forward like a seasoned hunter.

"Shush!" he exclaimed, turning toward me with his index finger on his lips.

Noko Mwini and I froze on our steps, strained our ears, but I still could hear nothing. *Mwini must be hearing voices,* I thought.

"Shush! Did you hear that noise?" he whispered

"What noise?" I whispered back.

"I can hear footsteps coming this way. Behind the bush now!" Noko Mwini quickly whispered.

Noko Mwini and I both scrambled to the safety of the bush. We instinctively dropped to the ground and lay flat on the muddy forest floor next to each other. From where we were hidden, we had a fairly good view of the path. We waited there motionless and in absolute silence. My heart was pounding hard against my chest. The sound of the footsteps grew louder as Houdini's towering figure came into full view. We looked at each other, heaved a sigh of relief, and smiled. We scrambled back to our feet to meet Houdini, who in turn nearly fainted when he heard the bush crackle under our weight.

Upon seeing us, Houdini put his hand on his chest, heaved a sigh of relief, shook his head, rubbed his temples, smiled, and came to greet us, and we started talking.

"My God! You nearly gave me a heart attack, guys," he sighed.

He nervously darted a glance around, rubbed his eyes, ran his hand over his receding hairline, scratched the back of his neck, nervously glanced around again, and whispered, "The enemies are based in Nkila-poste, and they're threatening to slaughter everybody in Mouyondzi."

"Oh really? Glad to know!" Noko Mwini smirked.

"This is no laughing matter, Mwini. We'd better start praying for mercy! Things will get pretty ugly soon," he warned.

"Where did you get the information from? And how reliable are your sources?" Noko Mwini inquired.

Noko Mwini was curious but didn't seem convinced by what Houdini was saying. I, on the other hand, was listening attentively, not knowing what to make of it.

"I have my sources, and they're reliable. The enemies are comprised mostly of foreign mercenaries hired by the new administration to hunt us down like wild animals and slaughter us with no mercy," he said, emphasizing his message by making a knife sign running across his neck.

"Hallelujah! That already makes me feel better!" Noko Mwini sarcastically exclaimed. He darted a quick "don't believe this nonsense" look toward me and focused his attention back on Houdini.

"Make fun of me now. But trust me, Mwini, we're about to endure tremendous hardships. Mark my words!" he confidently stated.

"I guess we'll all have to wait and see what happens then," replied Mwini, sounding serious this time.

"Needless to say, my comrades and I have put together a team of brave men ready to risk their lives for the security of others. We'll be circulating from camp to camp to keep our people informed on the position of the government forces. For our people, we're prepared to die serving them," he explained.

"I thank you and your comrades."

If you and your comrades didn't start the rebellion in the first place, we wouldn't be having this conversation, paranoid in the middle of nowhere, I thought.

The blunders of the few endangered the lives of the many. I was deeply frustrated that we were forced to hide indefinitely in the forests, hunted down by the government forces like wild animals, all for a movement we didn't endorse at all. The cold reality was a bitter pill to swallow. There we were, confused, forced out of our homes, talking to a former rebel and the root cause of our predicament. Houdini had a knack for finding people, I must admit. He would definitely have made an excellent tracker.

"Did you perhaps see my mother and the rest of the family?" Noko Mwini asked.

"Yes, I did. I helped your mother and others find a good hiding spot in Boussaka yesterday. You'll find them near the river Moukeri," he said, pointing us in the direction where my grandmother and the rest of our family members were.

Notwithstanding the source of the newly-acquired information, I still felt a little relieved that we at last had something that would help us plan our next move. Noko Mwini and I left Houdini and hurried down the winding path through the forest until we reached the site where my grandmother and other family members were hidden.

"What a relief! Thank you, sweet Lord, for protecting all my children and grandchildren!" my grandmother exclaimed with relief when she saw us. "Where are you camped? How are you keeping? Is everything fine?" She bombarded us with questions to which she didn't wait for answers.

My grandmother was pacing back and forth, her arms behind her back, folded and rested on her waist; every now and then she would stop for a second, raise her hands toward the sky, look up, mumble a prayer, and continue pacing aimlessly back and forth.

"We're just fine, Mum. You ought to stop worrying and stressing too much. Stress kills, you know," Noko Mwini warned.

"You have no idea what it is like to have children scattered all over the place in a time of serious trouble like this," she said with pity in her voice.

"Mum, we're not little children anymore; we can take care of ourselves. I want you to stop worrying, all right?" he reminded her, sounding a little annoyed.

"It's easy for you to say! Some day you'll understand when you have your own children," she said.

"Mum, stop worrying! Worries do nothing else but hurt your health!" he stormed and walked away.

My grandmother ignored her son's advice, looked lost in her thoughts as she turned her gaze toward the sky, mumbled something between her teeth, and continued pacing aimlessly back and forth in the tiny space they managed to clear. Everybody looked confused, despondent, and I could see defeat written all over their faces. I could read their thoughts and feel their pain as if it were my own. Sadly, there was nothing I could do except wait patiently for Providence to turn things around in our favor. We were all faced with the same enigma, unfairly trapped in the forests fighting for survival. It broke my spirit to find myself in a position where I couldn't really help. Noko Mwini and I talked to everybody, exchanged news, and quickly headed back to our refuge. In the meantime, my mum kept busy around camp. She got the fire going and borrowed utensils from our new neighbors. She managed to boil vegetables and mushrooms without salt.

"Hey guys! I made some food for us," she said.

"Where did you get these utensils and the fire from?" I asked.

"I borrowed them from the neighbors. Let's eat; Leolin and I are starving!"

My mother was quite resourceful, like most villagers there. Resourcefulness was a skill inherent for survival in the wild. I was happy our group had it in abundance. The meal she made looked like pea soup and tasted like wet cardboard. I was grateful for it and didn't hesitate to wolf it down, nonetheless. We ate for subsistence and I felt privileged to have something to eat. Leolin took one look at the food, made a face to express her disgust, refused to eat it and asked for a better meal.

"Mum, I don't like this food. I want something else," she cried.

As a three-year-old child, her young mind couldn't understand the gravity of the volatile situation we found ourselves in. My mum ventured out in the dark and somehow found some wild berries and fruit, which Leolin ended up eating. Time flew and the night was fast approaching. We inspected our camp to make sure there were no snakes lurking around before we all drifted off to sleep.

A GLIMMER OF HOPE

The sunrise looked majestic diffusing rays of pure light, which radiated through the forest canopy. A new day was dawning, and the forest came alive. Voices echoed around us as a cloud of smoke from newly-made fireplaces rose toward the sky. The sound of an axe or a machete cutting down shrubs, branches, or trees traveled through the woods. A new village comprising shapeless huts was emerging in the middle of the dense forest, and a united community of new nomads was born. Everybody helped each other as best they could. It felt like one big, loving, caring family.

In the meantime the enemies had parked their vehicles a few kilometers away from villages. They snuck up on people from village to village mercilessly, slaughtering them. Like a group of cunning thieves, they arrived in Nkenge unnoticed kicking doors open. They stormed into every hut, looking for any form of life to take away. To their surprise, Nkenge looked as desolate as a ghost town; the villagers had vanished into thin air. The enemies stood still for a while, straining their ears hoping to hear voices. They then resolved to walk to the hill on the outskirts of Nkenge where they had a fairly good view of the forest. They pointed their machine guns to the direction where the smoke was gracefully rising to the sky and opened fire. Everybody was caught off guard; we instinctively dropped to the ground, lay flat on the muddy forest floor, hurriedly put out the fire my mother struggled to get started, and quickly slithered through the bush for safety. Instructions were shouted to all and sundry in panic.

"Put out the fire! Pour water over it now!" somebody shouted.

"Get down on the ground immediately!" Noko Mwini commanded.

"Silence! Let's keep quiet!" my mother whispered.

Bullets whistled all over the place and the deafening sounds of machine guns continued to resonate through the whole forest. Humans, domestic, and wild animals fell quiet. We silently prayed for a ceasefire as lots of newly-built huts caught fire in the shooting. We all slithered deeper into the dense forest, trying to get as far away as we could from the shooting. I cried bitter tears, and laughed hysterically as if I had gone mad. *Is this a nightmare? Or is this really happening?* I asked myself. I couldn't wrap my head around the whole situation. My heart was racing, I was panting, beads of sweat were oozing out of my pores, the hair on my body stood up, and I was shaking uncontrollably. My mind was out of control as it started imagining horrible scenarios in which we'd be killed in the most gruesome way. *This could be the end of us,* I thought.

The shooting stopped as abruptly as it began. The enemies exhausted their ammunition for the day and returned to their base camp in Nkila-poste—at least, that's what we thought. They set huts and houses on fire on their way back and were obviously satisfied with their first shift at work. After the machine guns fell silent, we stayed hidden, silent, and almost catatonic for about an hour. We didn't know whether the enemies had left or if they were still in the vicinity, waiting for us to emerge out of our hiding spots so that they could slaughter us. There was absolute silence everywhere, which was worrying and frightening. Some villagers very carefully tiptoed their way back to the periphery of the village to see whether the enemies had left or not. From where they hid, they caught a glimpse of the government forces walking away from the village through the main dirt road. They lay there, well hidden and motionless, for more than twenty minutes to ensure that the enemies hadn't left spies behind lurking around the village. One by one, they carefully circled around the four corners of the village, scanning each one of them for potential danger. They then walked into the village to assess the damage. Houses and huts were riddled with bullet holes, thatched roofs set on fire, windows and doors were kicked off their hinges, glass was shattered, and anything of value was looted. The enemies defecated and urinated in some huts. Our informants came back to the forest, where the rest of us were waiting and invoking the ancestors' assistance in silence, to announce that the enemies had returned to their base camp. We finally scrambled to our feet, left our temporary hiding spots, congregated in family groups, and started waddling back to our respective locations. Our new self-appointed informants were mostly former rebels. I suppose they were trying to redeem themselves by volunteering to keep everybody in hiding informed of the enemies' whereabouts. I still resented their presence anywhere near me because their stupidity and recklessness had put our lives in danger. Nonetheless, I had neither the power nor the authority to do anything about it.

Silence can sometimes be the voice of wisdom, I reminded myself.

Shortly after my family and I had gathered at our site trying to figure out the way forward, Houdini showed up.

"Pretty fucked up, huh?" he chuckled.

Noko Mwini was leaning against a tree, staring into the sky before him, his arms folded on his chest. He looked pensive and didn't turn around to look at Houdini.

"What do you mean?" Noko Mwini rhetorically asked with a hint of irritation in his voice.

"Being hunted down like wild animals by cold-blooded killers in our own backyard," Houdini lamented.

"Didn't we see it coming?" Noko Mwini snapped.

Houdini ignored Noko Mwini's question, then turned his attention to me. He was stroking his long beard, looking directly at me with a smirk on his face, and said, "I guess we all screwed up, huh? It looks like we'll have to put up with these bastards for a while."

I was sitting on the ground with my legs crossed, my hands

clasped together behind my head, staring at the shrubs in front of me, and lost in my own thoughts.

"Didn't you give the enemies a solemn invitation to invade this land through the pathetic rebellion?" I stormed.

With my cheek resting on my left hand, I grabbed a broken dry twig with my right hand and scribbled illegible words on the yellow and dusty ground.

"Forget the university gentleman. We all screwed up!" he blurted.

I didn't know what else to say or how to answer him. So I kept quiet and continued staring at the shrubs in front of me. I was trying to zone out for a moment. Houdini was partly right, because the present looked chaotic and the future didn't look promising at all. However, I didn't need anybody to remind me of the misery of our present reality. Instead, I needed the voice of hope to help strengthen my waning faith. The more often he opened his mouth to speak, the more I understood why my mother didn't like him at all. Noko Mwini, on the other hand, knew how to deal with him. He interacted with him with tact and patience. He left the tree he was leaning on earlier and started slowly pacing back and forth, looking downcast but still pensive and attentive to the conversation.

"Why is that?" Noko Mwini asked.

Houdini suddenly wiped the smirk off his face, darted a glance around the site, looked serious, lowered his voice, sounding like he was whispering, and said, "I think you haven't grasped the gravity of the situation yet."

"And you have because?"

There was a quick pause. Houdini didn't answer Noko Mwini's question, started stroking his beard again, looked up into the sky, and tried to gather his thoughts.

"This predicament has nothing to do with my nephew and university," Noko Mwini continued.

"Look around you, Mwini. What do you see, huh? I don't

know about you but I certainly don't see any light at the end of the tunnel," he said.

"You have every right to be pessimistic about the current circumstances, Houdini. But I believe in divine destiny and I'm going to stay faithful about the future."

"Divine destiny, Mwini? Seriously? That's wishful thinking, brother," he smirked, shaking his head in disbelief.

Noko Mwini suddenly stopped pacing back and forth, leaned back on the tree, scratched his head, wore a serious look on his face, looked Houdini in the eye, and calmly stressed, "Let me tell you this, my dear friend: divine destiny is a written future that nobody or no circumstances can stop."

"Keep telling yourself that, Mwini," he giggled and continued shaking his head in disbelief.

"You wouldn't understand even if I tried explaining it," Noko Mwini said.

"Don't be irrational, Mwini! This mess is rearranging divine destiny; it is turning everything upside down in our lives."

"I'm being irrational? Joining a pathetic rebellion certainly was irrational!" He laughed out loud.

"We were trying to set you free from a dictatorial regime, remember that!" he snapped.

"Did I hit a nerve there, Houdini? Huh?" he smirked.

"You can make fun of me now but remember what I said earlier."

"I have no room in my mind for doubt and unbelief," Noko Mwini emphasized.

"Keep dreaming, Mwini. I honestly don't see how we can get out of this ongoing killing game alive."

"You may not see or believe it, but I beg to differ. We'll make it alive and live to tell the tale, believe it or not!" he asserted.

Noko Mwini's last words silenced Houdini and made him leave quickly. I really liked the way Noko Mwini handled Houdini.

BRAVING DANGER

My mother and Leolin rejoined us and we briefly loitered about. Darkness was progressively settling in and Noko Mwini was about to rush back to the village to collect the items we needed. Despite my strong opposition the day earlier, I hesitantly offered to accompany him.

"It's getting dark very quickly. I must shoot back to the village and pick up some of our things," Noko Mwini said.

"I'm coming with you," I offered.

"No, you are not!" my mother interrupted in a commanding voice.

"Let him come with me, sister. We'll be all right," Noko Mwini pleaded.

"Forget it! You're not taking my son there! I'd rather go with you," my mother offered.

"Mum, you can't go back there. Give us a list of what you need, and we'll bring it to you."

She placed her left hand on my shoulder, looked me in the eye, and sternly said with authority, "Listen to me my son: you stay here! You're not going anywhere near that village. Do you understand me?"

"The enemies left a long time ago, Mum," I replied in a subdued voice.

"You're not going anywhere! Do you understand me? I'm not making the same mistake as your father!" she stormed.

I could not persuade my mother to allow me to accompany Noko Mwini to the village. I felt so frustrated that she was so overly protective of me. I saw myself as a man who could take care of himself. I guess in my mother's eyes I was still her little boy whom she had to continuously protect from a dangerous world. Noko Mwini and my mother wasted no more time; they quickly trotted back to Nkenge. Leolin was starving and her stomach was churning. She began to cry for food.

"Yaya, I'm hungry. I want food! Give me food! I'm hungry!" Leolin cried, looking up at me with expectancy in her eyes.

There was absolutely nothing to eat, and it was too dark for me to venture out anywhere in the forest in search of food. Again, I felt powerless, useless, frustrated, and defeated. I picked her up; she wrapped her arms around my neck, and rested her head on my shoulder. I slowly paced around, back and forth, whispering comforting words to her until she finally fell asleep. I waited with bated breath for Noko Mwini and my mother to come back. Every minute that passed with no sign of them, I grew worried and afraid that something terrible might have happened.

What's taking them so long to come back? I wondered.

Noko Mwini and my mother finally made it back safely. They collected as much stuff as they could, loaded everything into baskets, and carried it to our refuge.

"What took you so long, guys?" I asked.

They both ignored my question, set the heavy baskets down, and my mum said, "Help us offload. We have a lot to do."

We got the fire going and my mother made a decent meal consisting of smoked fish and vegetables cooked with palm oil. Considering our circumstances, I felt privileged to have a decent meal with salt. And it was a delectable meal, which Leolin and I wolfed down until we were fully satisfied. We now had the basic resources at our disposal, which made life in the Boussaka a little easier for a few days. The evening was quiet and very dark; there were no stars, no moon shining through the forest canopy. We sat around the fire and talked for hours.

"Tomorrow at the break of dawn, we have to leave this refuge for the day to go and hide somewhere else," Noko Mwini advised.

"Do you think they'll come back to Nkenge tomorrow?" I asked.

"It is hard to tell because they seem very unpredictable. What we know for sure is that they're trained killers deployed to this part of the country to kill anybody they come across," Noko Mwini explained

"We don't deserve this punishment. This is absolutely unacceptable!" my mother said.

"Where are these trained killers from?" I inquired.

"What difference does it make? They're simply killers, wherever they hail from," Noko Mwini replied.

"Lord, have mercy!" my mother said, making the cross sign.

"Our main concern is survival. How do we survive during this manhunt? That is the main puzzle we must try to solve," Noko Mwini added.

I was growing sick and tired of discussing the same topic over and over again. I missed my simple life in Pointe-Noire, my father, my sisters, and my friends. I missed playing soccer with my friends every afternoon in the sandy streets of Voungou. I missed the beautiful sandy beach in Pointe-Noire. I missed everybody and everything in Pointe-Noire. I earnestly wanted to go home immediately. On the edge of the mattress I closed my eyes to call upon God, to ask for divine protection. I recited a prayer in my heart, and promised to become a better person if the Lord let me and my family live through the valley of the shadow of death. I stretched my body full length on the mattress, drew the blanket up to my face, and drifted off to sleep.

STRATEGIZING AND PLANNING

At about 3 am my mother woke me. It was time to prepare ourselves because we had to go and hide somewhere we deemed safer. I got up and poured some water from the twenty-five liter drum into a small plastic bucket. I cleaned myself up quickly and joined Noko Mwini, my mother, and Leolin around the fire. We all shared the leftovers from last night's dinner. We ate our meal fast and in silence. At 4 am we packed all of our belongings away. Half an hour later, we started the long walk toward our refuge for the day. We trudged up the hills, down the valleys, across the streams until we stopped in front of some thick bushes. We crept through a cluster of abundant shrubs and lay flat on our bellies. We stayed hidden in that position for hours, waiting for danger to recede. The rattling sounds of machine guns tore through the air for most of the afternoon. Darkness was closing in, the machine guns fell silent, and we judged it safe enough to leave our daytime hiding spot. So we rose to our feet and made our way back to camp.

The following day, we religiously followed the same routine as the day before. The government forces didn't come to Nkenge. Most people wondered whether the move was part of their strategy or if they'd just taken the day off. We were all confused and didn't really know what to make of it. On our way back to camp, I didn't hesitate to express my discontent about how overly careful we were being.

"I think we're being way too careful about the whole situation," I started.

"This is not a game! This is a matter of life or death, young man!" Noko Mwini said.

"I don't disagree with you that this is a matter of life and death. But honestly, do we have to wake up very early in the morning daily and start rushing across the forest? I asked, sounding a little annoyed.

"The rigorous routine we've been following will keep us safe. We can't afford to relax and forget that we're being hunted by merciless killers who are determined to carry out their mission to the letter," he stressed.

"The enemies might have decided not to kill innocent people. They might have a conscience after all," I said.

"How can the enemies distinguish rebels from the innocent? Huh? The enemies are trained killers. I wouldn't be naïve enough to even think for one second they're here on a humanitarian mission."

"They might have had a change of heart. They didn't show up anywhere near Nkenge today."

"Don't be naïve, my nephew. Those bastards are not to be taken lightly. They'll come back to cause more damage, mark my words," he ended.

My mother didn't join the conversation; with Leolin in tow, she walked in silence, lost in her own thoughts.

"Mum, is everything ok?" I asked.

"I'm fine, thank you, my son. I'm just tired and I don't feel like talking. It's been a long day," she replied.

"Yes, it has been a really long day."

We made it back at about four in the afternoon. We all felt and looked exhausted from the long and steep walk. However, we had to get to work straight away because we had a lot to do. There was never time to take a break; there was always something going on. We retrieved our belongings from where we'd hidden them in the morning, made a fire, and the cooking began. We made a lot of food that would last us at least three days: beans and rice, salted and dry fish, vegetables, cassava leaves with palm oil, potatoes, etc. We all worked meticulously as a team, and a few hours later the food was ready, packed in plastic bags. We had dinner around the fire and walked down to the stream to refill water bottles and to wash ourselves. At night the forest came alive: people talked aloud, kids cried and laughed and so on. But in the daytime, there was absolute silence everywhere.

Despite my discussion with Noko Mwini over our careful approach toward survival, we religiously followed the same routine the day after. We headed back to the same spot and hid there until late in the afternoon.

For the second day in a row, the enemies didn't visit Nkenge. This led some villagers to surmise that it was safe enough to return to their homes. I felt the same way, as the poor living conditions were beginning to take their toll on me. I wanted to walk back to Nkenge straight away. But for my family's extremely careful strategy, I would have followed those who decided to go back. Noko Mwini was quick to warn, "This is a trap! Those returning to their homes are putting themselves in tremendous danger."

"How do you know that?" I asked.

"I have a hunch. We can't return now; it is too soon for us to go back," Noko Mwini stressed.

"Many people are going back. Why can't we go back?"

"There is a silent voice that speaks to all of us every time we're to make a crucial decision. We usually ignore that silent voice and end up suffering the consequences," Noko Mwini philosophized.

"What is your point, uncle?"

"Never follow blindly and naïvely what other people do. Instead, do what you perceive to be right at a crucial time like this."

"You mean to tell that we can't return yet because of some silent voice whispering revelations in your ears?"

"That's correct, nephew. You just know when something doesn't feel right. Going back to our homes at this stage doesn't feel right. I can't explain but I just know it."

"We might never go back if we place our trust in a silent voice or a hunch," I said.

"I promise you that we'll go back some day. But today is definitely not that day. We should be very careful."

"Don't you think we're playing it too safe?"

"We live once to die forever. We can't be too casual when it is a matter of life or death. We're not going back yet!" he stormed.

"Okay! Let your will be done," I frustratedly conceded.

I began to think that Noko Mwini was a coward. He was trying to hold back my mother, Leolin, and me, to keep us from taking the proper course of action whenever necessary. Not even a day passed until the enemies graced Nkenge with a surprise visit. They parked their vehicles miles away, snuck into villages, and wreaked havoc. They launched a couple of grenades into the center of Nkenge, and the detonation drove villagers out of their homes. The enemies' machine guns rattled and rumbled throughout the village. My family and I lay hidden. We could hear the thunderous sounds of their machine guns as if they were firing them a hundred yards away. Unlucky villagers, mostly elderly people and the physically handicapped, who could not escape fast enough got caught in the blaze and met their Maker. Dead bodies were riddled with bullet wounds beyond recognition. Some escaped, seriously injured, and bled all the way down to the forest. Nkenge experienced the wrath and cruelty of the oppressors. Any confusion the villagers entertained in their minds about the enemies' intentions in Mouyondzi was clarified in the most dramatic way. Everybody learned the hard way that returning to their homes prematurely was a costly mistake.

Around three in the afternoon, the enemies returned to their base camp. The forest was filled with cries and traditional songs of mourning; everybody was grieving for the dead. My family's extra careful strategy helped us survive to see another day.

The noise of mourning reached our safe haven. We picked ourselves up and followed the direction where the sounds of distress were coming from. I felt guilty for trying to persuade my family to return to the village too early. *It was selfish of me to want to put myself before anybody else,* I thought. I couldn't look Noko Mwini in the eye. He read my thoughts and tried to make me feel better.

"Don't beat yourself up, nephew. What matters right now is that we're still alive. We have survived through the horrors of today to see another day. One day at a time," he said.

I didn't have anything else to add to that so I continued to walk in silence. As we got closer to our hiding spot, cries and songs of mourning grew louder and louder. Leolin and I walked straight back to camp while my mother and Noko Mwini went toward the mourners.

Weeks elapsed and the enemies continued to hunt people down with the same motivation as they did when they first took control of the district. They continued to kill people here and there. On numerous occasions, crazy rebels would fire a few shots in the air with their AK47s to exasperate the enemies. They would respond by raining bullets at anything that moved. Day by day life became more challenging for all of us on the run. Everybody was running out of resources: salt, matches, paraffin, medicines, etc. As a result, the weak began to succumb to all sorts of diseases: diarrhoea, malaria, tick bite fever, yellow fever…all the fevers you can think of.

The premises of a primary school in Mayalama, a small village west of Nkila-poste, served as a refuge for about sixty people. One morning the enemies snuck into the village, closed in on the villagers, caught everybody who was hiding at the school, and slaughtered each one of them. To this day, I still don't understand why men are so cruel to one another. The Mayalama carnage sent a strong message of fear everywhere across the whole district. Everybody I came across that day looked utterly shattered, downcast, and despondent.

Death felt closer and more real to everybody. People migrated around in the quest to find more secure hiding spots, as did my family.

A TRIP TO MOUZANGA

Kihoulou felt unsafe in Nkenge. Day by day, she wanted to go to Mouzanga and stay with her parents. She talked to Noko Moussoki about her plan.

"Ya Moussoki, I must rejoin my parents. I feel unsafe here," Kihoulou confided.

Noko Moussoki felt torn. He didn't really know what to do but understood Kihoulou because he empathized with her.

"I don't really want you to leave, but I do understand. You can take the kids with you," he reluctantly said.

"Okay! Thank you for understanding!"

"When things get a little quieter, I'll be coming up to Mouzanga for a visit. May the ancestors be with you!" he said as he bid them goodbye.

Kihoulou and the children left Nkenge at once. Noko Moussoki found himself in a tricky situation. Circumstances had forced his family to separate. Days passed; he could no longer stand it. He had to go and see his family.

"Mum, I'm going to visit my wife and kids in Mouzanga," Noko Moussoki said.

"What? Have you lost your mind? I don't want you to go there!" my grandmother emphasized.

"I have to go and see them, Mum. I can't spend another day without knowing how they are," he explained.

"Kihoulou and my granddaughters are with their family. I believe it's safer in Mouzanga than it is here. I have no doubt in my mind they're well and safe where they are," my grandmother reasoned.

"How would you know that? I miss my wife and kids! I have to go there and see for myself that they're safe and well," he insisted.

My grandmother pleaded with him not to go anywhere. She begged him to stay put like everybody else.

"I'm begging you not to venture out of Boussaka. Stay put until things slow down a little," she pleaded.

"I'm not a kid anymore; you don't have to protect me. I can take care of myself. My mind is already made up, Mum. I'm leaving immediately," he reiterated.

My grandmother got the message loud and clear, and said, "You don't have to lecture me. I do understand, Moussoki. May the ancestors be with you all the way!"

He took off for a long walk to Mouzanga, which he covered in about an hour and fifteen minutes. He reconnected with his wife and kids. To his surprise, he noticed that villagers there weren't hiding in the forests. They'd decided to remain in the village despite the impending danger. They assumed that Mouzanga was too far for the enemies to reach. He spent half of the day with his family and started to make his way back in the afternoon. His eleven-year-old son Ndeke insisted on joining him.

"Papa, I don't want to stay here anymore. Can I come with you, please?" Ndeke asked

"Ya Moussoki, you should take him with you. He has done nothing but complain ever since we got here," Kihoulou revealed.

"It sounds like I don't have a choice, do I? Come on, Ndeke. Let's go then," he said.

A young man called Nioka, who had to go to Nkenge for some reason, also ended up tagging along. They left Mouzanga and passed through Mpandi. It was about three o'clock in the afternoon when they got to Mouandi, a small village five kilometers west of Nkenge. Noko Moussoki, Ndeke, and Nioka walked carefully and silently through the forests behind the villages. They only took the main road each time they hit a dead end in the forests. Halfway through Mouandi, Nioka told them that he had an upset stomach and needed to make a quick stop.

"Go on, guys. I need the toilet urgently," Nioka said.

"Are you all right? We can wait for you, if you like," Noko Moussoki offered.

"I'm ok. I'll catch up with you in a second," Nioka replied. He quickly disappeared behind some thick bushes edging the main dirt road. In the meantime, Noko Moussoki and Ndeke continued to edge their way down the road in silence. Suddenly, the enemy emerged out of nowhere and closed in on the two of them. Noko Moussoki and Ndeke tried to run but froze in their tracks when they heard the clicking noise of the enemy's gun.

"Freeze! Stop right there! Don't run!" the enemy shouted.

Noko Moussoki and Ndeke had hit a snag. He began regretting not listening to his mother. The enemy was towering over them, pointing the gun at them, with his finger on the trigger, repeating, "You bandido! Rebelde! Huh? Huh?"

"M-m-my na-na-name is Moussoki, an-n-d this is my son. I-I-I work f-for the national M-Metrorail Co-company as a tech-technician," he stuttered.

"You no technician! You lie! You lie! Me know you lie! You rebelde! Rebelde! Bandido! Infiltrado!"

"I-I'm not a liar; I a-m-m telling the tru-truth," he continued to stutter with tears welling up in his eyes.

"Where you going? Why you no work? Rebelde! Infiltrado!" he yelled.

"My s-s-son and-d-d I are go-go-going ho-ho-ho-me," Noko Moussoki stuttered, almost whimpering for mercy.

"Shut up! You bandido! Infiltrado!" he shouted angrily.

"Please! I-I-I'm be-begging you! Please! Ha-ha-ha-have mer-mercy!" he stuttered.

"Inflitrado! Bandido! Rebelde!" the enemy shouted.

At hearing those last words, Noko Moussoki anticipated what was about to happen. Their fates were sealed. The enemy pointed the gun to Noko Moussoki's right cheek as his son stood beside him, awaiting their fate with bitter tears streaming down his cheeks. He pulled the trigger. The bullet pierced through the right cheek and blasted the left cheek and jaw open. Noko Moussoki crumbled to the ground convulsing and collapsed unconscious onto the gravel road, soaked in his own blood. Ndeke fell instinctively alongside his father, held his breath, and played dead. Nioka, now aware of what was happening, took off running, trying to retrace his steps through the forests. The enemies that were hidden on both sides of the main road sprinted after him. They fired a few rounds in the direction where they believed Nioka was escaping. They scanned the area and found nobody. Nioka had vanished into thin air. They came back where Noko Moussoki and Ndeke lay unconscious and kicked Noko Moussoki's seriously wounded body and Ndeke to make sure they were dead. Both remained motionless. The enemies assumed that they were both dead and left them there. When Ndeke realized that the enemies were out of sight and long gone, he grabbed his father's right hand and squeezed it to wake him. He called out to his father, who lay still with blood all over him. In vain, Ndeke cried out for help.

"Papa! Papa! Papa! Wake up! Wake up! Somebody help! Help me please!" he cried out.

Noko Moussoki miraculously rose to his feet. With both hands, he held his disjointed jaw together and ran straight into the forest toward Nkenge. Ndeke raced after his father through a winding path where some people of good faith helped them convey the message to my grandmother and the rest of the family.

"Why me? Why my son?" my grandmother cried.

The whole family was crushed and my poor grandmother couldn't stop crying. She would pace around, up and down, sit down on the floor, cry, stand up, raise her hands toward the sky, question the ancestors, and implore them for help. She cursed the enemies and cried until she lost her voice.

Noko Moussoki needed immediate medical attention and possibly reconstructive surgery. The damage to his face looked scary. The struggle was real! Through her connections, my grandmother managed to get a doctor who was hiding in Mouandi to come and examine Noko Moussoki. The doctor took a look at him and suggested that he be taken to a hospital overseas if or when all survived. In the meantime, we turned to traditional medicine. Noko Moussoki was in excruciating pain. His cries broke our hearts, shattered our spirits, and killed our morale. Our hope for survival was waning fast.

IN HINDSIGHT

There was nothing else we could do for Noko Moussoki other than offer him our emotional support. We left my grandmother's camp and headed back to our own. That evening the mood was down, and our morale had hit a new low. We were restless, wallowing in self-pity, and slipping deeper into depression. We sat around the fire as we did every night. This time we had no appetite and everybody was lost in their own thoughts. Leolin was already sleeping. Noko Mwini, my mother, and I sat in silence. But this was the type of silence that was expressive. We were on the same wavelength and could read each other's thoughts. Death felt more real and closer than ever before.

"This is why I'm furious at your father!" my mother snapped.

"Mum, can't you let it go, please?" I said, almost pleading.

"You don't get it, do you? Huh?" she asked.

"Everybody makes mistakes sometimes," I said.

"You've always tried to defend your father. But let me tell you one thing: this is unacceptable and I'm very angry with him! What happened to Moussoki might happen to us anytime!"

I kept quiet. I didn't want to say anything else for fear of making her angrier than she already was.

"Your father has two rental properties in Pointe-Noire, one in Brazzaville, and possibly some more nobody else knows about since he is very secretive about his wealth. Do you mean to tell me that he doesn't have enough money to send you to university?"

"I-I don't know what t-to say, Mum," I stuttered.

I avoided eye contact with my mother, but I could feel her

eyes boring a hole into my head. *Do I make this woman angry because I look like my father and also have his first and last names?* I wondered.

Noko Mwini tried to come to my rescue and said, "Sister, nobody knew that all this would be happening right now."

"Stay out of this, Mwini!" my mother retorted.

Noko Mwini got the message, walked away, and went straight to lie down. My mother was still shaking with anger.

"He always has money for his nephews, nieces, brothers, sisters, and mistresses. But to send his own son to university, he suddenly has no money! And here we are, stranded in the forest, being hunted down by savages. We're probably going to die here soon. And you expect me to be okay with your father's reckless behavior?"

There was nothing else for me to say or do. So I picked myself up, walked to the shelter, lay down, and drifted off to sleep. My mother, on the other hand, still angry, stayed up late by the fire.

FLIRTING WITH DANGER

My younger sister Mouesse was heavily pregnant in Kimfinkou, a tiny village south of Nkenge, and my mother could not bear the thought of leaving Mouesse in the care of her in-laws. Despite what happened to her brother, my mother was still adamant about visiting Mouesse once or twice a week. Noko Mwini and I tried to talk her out of it, but she would not change her mind and refused to listen to reason.

"Don't do this to us, Mum, please!" I pleaded.

"Why not? Mouesse is my daughter. I have to look after her," my mother said.

"Noko Moussoki wouldn't have been shot if he stayed in one place and listened to Grandma," I reminded her.

At the mention of her brother's name, my mother fell silent for a minute, and I thought I'd hit the right note and she was reconsidering her decision because the risk was massive and real.

"Mouesse has a loving and caring family around her. They won't abandon her," Noko Mwini added.

"I don't trust those people; they are a breed of snakes! Mouesse told me all about them," she retorted.

"Mum, why can't you listen?"

"What do you expect me to do, huh? Do you expect me to sit here and do nothing because of these bloody enemies?"

"What about Leolin and me? Are we not your children too? Don't you think we also need you?"

"You're not pregnant, are you? Your sister needs me! I'm

ordering you to stop telling me what I can or cannot do," she snapped and walked away.

I knew my mother had already made up her mind about visiting Mouesse. Any attempt to talk her out of it made her even more determined to go there. I could only hope and pray that nothing horrible would befall her. On the following day, my mother got up very early in the morning and trekked through the forests to get to Kimfinkou. Noko Mwini, Leolin, and I followed our usual routine. Noko Mwini confided that he would have to make some big changes if Mouesse came to join us.

"Your sister is heavily pregnant, and from your mother's reaction yesterday, Mouesse will end up here with us soon. If or when it happens, I'll leave and find someplace else to hide," he said.

"Why do you want to do that?" I inquired.

"A pregnant woman will certainly slow us down. Moreover, once the baby is born, it could be very easy for the enemies to locate our position," he explained.

I felt a little sad that he was to leave our group sometime soon. But I also understood that he was only trying to survive by any means, like the rest of us, and he was eager to take whatever action necessary to achieve that goal. However, I could never follow him and abandon my mother and sisters.

"Whatever happens, I can't leave my family. I'll stay right here with them until the end," I said.

"I understand, my nephew."

Every second that passed felt like I was pricked with a sharp needle. I waited with bated breath for my mother to return safe and sound. Worried couldn't even begin to describe how I was feeling inside. I took care of Leolin, however, as best as I could. Noko Mwini and I spent the time whispering to each other. Late in the afternoon we returned to our camp. A few minutes later, to our relief, my mother arrived back unharmed.

"How was your trip to Kimfinkou, Mum?" I sighed

"Oh, it was fine! I used shortcuts through the forests to get there. Not even once did I have to edge down the main dirt road," she explained.

"Is Mouesse all right? What did she say?"

"Your sister is fine. But I'm going back there tomorrow; she needs my help."

Noko Mwini was sitting under our shelter, listening to the conversation, and shaking his head every now and then in disbelief. He knew not to break in on a serious conversation that involved my mother and her children.

"Why?" I asked.

"You and I already had this conversation, don't you remember? I'm not going to repeat myself, for you already know where I stand on this," she emphasized.

"Can't you ask Mouesse's husband to drop her off here?"

"Fine! I'll talk to him about it tomorrow!" she replied, throwing her hands in the air in frustration.

"Mum, you must persuade him to do it sooner rather than later. The sooner you stop going there the better it is for all of us," I stressed.

"Must we have the same discussion for you to understand that I'll never abandon Mouesse?" she asked, looking at me defiantly.

I avoided eye contact with her, looked down at the floor, and said, "Under normal circumstances, I wouldn't be here and we wouldn't be having this discussion. I'm concerned about you getting shot at…"

"You wouldn't be here in the first place if your crazy father didn't send you here! So please stop telling me what to do," she interjected.

"As soon as this persecution is over, I'm going back to Pointe-Noire. I won't spend another second in this godforsaken land. I'll pack up my things and leave right away," I stormed and walked away.

I was fed up with my mother's stubbornness; I was frustrated and couldn't take it anymore. I felt like running away without looking back. It was nerve-wracking. I couldn't believe that my mother learned nothing from what had recently happened to her brother. I felt as though there was an evil force fueling my mother's decision to turn a deaf ear to common sense.

At the break of dawn, my mother left once again for Kimfinkou. At about 9am she decided to trek back, although she knew how great a risk she was running. She ran into two of her acquaintances heading in the same direction. They all got together and continued to make their way back. My mother and her walking companions got to a stretch of the path where they had to cut across the main dirt road to connect with the forest leading back to Nkenge. No sooner did they get halfway across the road than they heard a metallic click and an unfamiliar, deep, raspy and loud voice shout, "Stop! Stop right there! Don't move!"

My mother and her walking companions took off running into the forest. They sprinted as fast as they could and didn't look back. The enemy chased after them while firing multiple shots in their direction. Fortunately, he failed to hit his targets. My mother and her walking companions survived to see another day. She got back to camp panting, trying to gasp out words to explain what she'd just experienced.

"The enemy…t-tried…t-to…" she panted and stuttered.

I held her by the hand and led her to sit down on a dry tree stump. I crouched beside her, placed my left hand on her back, and handed her a glass of water.

"Sit down, Mum. Have a glass of water," I offered.

Beads of sweat trickled down her face. She looked utterly shocked, like somebody who has seen a ghost. She gulped down the water, heaved a sigh of relief, paused, took a deep breath, and finally began to speak.

"I nearly got killed today," she panted.

"Oh my God! What happened, Mum?" I inquired.

"The enemies tried to catch us between Kimfinkou and Nkenge. They opened fire as we took off running at full speed into the forest," she explained.

"Are you all right? Did they follow you here?" I asked.

"Yes I'm all right, just shaken. I'm certain that we were not followed. They don't know these forests like I do," she said.

I didn't want to tell her that I told her this would happen, that I had been right all along. I was just relieved that she was all right. We all were. Before I could change the subject, Noko Mwini interrupted me.

"Sister, I know how much you want to look after your pregnant daughter. However, this is certainly not the right time to play super mum. Moussoki's case is a permanent reminder to all of us to be extra careful during these dark days," he reasoned.

"I spoke to Mouesse's husband. He agreed to the idea of her coming here to stay with us. He promised to bring her tomorrow or the day after," she ended.

We all felt relieved that she finally came to her senses and was going to do the right thing.

The following day, we got up early like we normally did and retreated to our safe haven. In those dark days, we moved around so often that at some stage I thought we would end up in a different country! From where we hid, we could hear the enemies' machine guns rattling away. They were in the area firing shots in all directions as they always did. We got so used to hearing the sounds of machine guns that we grew unfazed by them. But we still acted carefully and couldn't afford to relax. We waited there patiently until the shooting stopped and made our way back to camp. At about 6pm Mouesse's husband dropped her off, as promised. We were all relieved and happy to be reunited with Mouesse. We briefly chatted with my brother-in-law, thanked him, and said goodbye to him.

"Welcome to the woods, sister!" I smiled, my face beaming with joy.

"Thanks. How is everybody doing?" Mouesse asked.

"Long time, no see! How are you feeling, little sister?" I asked.

"I'm exhausted from the long walk. We could have come earlier, but the enemies were all over Kimfinkou," she informed me.

"Wow! These enemies aren't showing any sign of slowing down, are they?" I said.

"Nope. They're getting more and more ruthless day by day... it's scary!"

"Mouesse, did you hear anything?" Noko Mwini asked.

"Not particularly— just rumors here and there. Today the enemies caught Kouamoussou's father and butchered him savagely with machetes like a wild animal! I'm at a loss for words," Mouesse said, nodding in disbelief.

"Mouesse, you said something about the rumors," Noko Mwini said.

"Yes, they're confusing and contradictory. I don't know what to believe anymore. Some say the struggle will end soon, whereas others say something different. Everybody seems to have something to say, which in truth lacks substance."

Noko Mwini slowly started massaging his chin with hand. He paused, closed his eyes for a second, sighed, scratched his head, and said, "What a terrible situation we find ourselves in! You and your husband lived in Bouansa during the fleeting reign of the rebels," he added.

"Yes, we did," she replied, nodding.

My jaw dropped open in surprise. I couldn't believe what I was hearing. I didn't want to interrupt Noko Mwini, so I waited for him finish what he had to say or ask Mouesse.

"How did you survive in such a place full of drama all the time?" Noko Mwini asked.

"My husband was running a tavern near the train station, and he got acquainted with most rebels. He treated them so well that they liked him and never bothered us. They even kept us informed on the progress of the rebellion and the position of the government troops."

My mother joined in as I was about to say something and said in disgust, "I can't believe that your husband made friends with those cold-blooded killers!"

"He didn't have a choice. Making friends with the rebels

was the only way for him to keep his business safe. Besides, his tavern had been running long before the rebellion started. He grew emotionally attached to it and couldn't afford to lose it," she explained.

"Wow! I can't believe this! You were living in Bouansa before the rebellion?"

"That's correct, brother. Why?"

"I was nearly stranded there. A young soldier on the train robbed me of my money. I had to beg and negotiate my way to Nkila-poste," I explained.

"Oh! That's too bad! If only you had known that my husband and I lived near Bouansa train station," she said.

"Yes! It's a pity that I had no idea! Anyway, I spoke to a taxi driver who happened to be Papa Ndazet's friend. The man was kind enough to help me out."

My mum kept busy around camp in the meantime, making food for all of us.

"Guys, the food is ready. Come and eat; you can catch up later," she said.

We all sat around the fire as usual and had dinner as a family. I was so happy to see Mouesse, to talk to her, and to know that my mother would no longer go back and forth between Nkenge and Kimfinkou. Noko Mwini didn't leave our camp straight away. I had my fingers crossed in hope that he wouldn't leave our group even when the baby was born. Days turned into weeks, but nothing changed in our favor. The government forces continued hunting people down and slaughtering them left, right and center. The more we prayed to Heaven for peace, the worse the situation grew.

"Will things ever change for us?" my mother asked.

"Let's not lose our faith in the Man above," I said.

"In times like these, it is hard for one's faith not to falter," she continued.

"We have nothing to lose if we believe and stay optimistic.

We have already made it this far. I believe Providence is arranging destiny in our favor," Noko Mwini comforted.

Due to the shortage of food, we were restricted to a meager diet of leaves, roots, berries, and fruit. Meat was hard to come by. Farmers had to put their livestock down or leave them behind. We had to settle for whatever we were lucky to find. I remember one day my cousins and I walked a few kilometers, scanning the forest for food. We saw a field mouse sneaking into a dark hole. We tiptoed closer to the hole and placed a stone over it. With hoes and machetes, we dug with determination, however solid the ground felt. We caught all six field mice. We were very delighted with our catch that day and could put some meat on the table. The longer we were forced to live in the forest, the sharper our survival skills got.

Another day, on our way to the stream nearby, we stumbled upon a dead sheep. The sight of a dead sheep on our path looked like a blessing from the sky! We felt that Heaven's angels were finally smiling down on us. I picked up the dead sheep without hesitation, slung it over my shoulders, and carried it to our camp. My cousins and I worked on the dead animal with diligence and made a delectable meal out of it, which the entire family feasted on. It was by far the most delicious meal I had during our time in the forest. We all learned to appreciate so many things in life we had taken for granted.

ON THE MOVE AGAIN

According to the traditional midwife who came to examine her, Mouesse's delivery date was nearing. We decided to change locations to welcome the baby. Noko Mwini seized the opportunity and said, ""The time has come for me to look for another hiding spot. God willing, we'll meet again when or if we survive. Do take care of yourselves. And may God himself protect us."

His departure made me feel a little sad. I cherished the time I spent in his company. I learned a few survival skills by watching and working alongside him. His knowledge, wisdom, and positive energy rubbed off on me. But it was time to move on and embrace the new. I felt that I had definitely graduated and was ready to successfully navigate my way around the dangers of life in the wild and continue eluding the enemies.

My mother and I trekked deeper through the forest looking for where we believed to be safest. We settled for a spot beside a stream. We got to work right away. Equipped with a machete and hoes, we cleared the area of thorn bushes, twigs, and vines. We had grown sick and tired of being hunted down, forced to abandon every shelter we ever built. Therefore, we decided to keep things simple this time.

"Four poles to support the roof, and that's it," my mother said.

"I'll get the poles, dig four holes, and we can put the shelter in place," I added.

My mother and I worked fast, and the shelter was standing after about half an hour. We carried all of our belongings to the new location. At the end of day, we felt so exhausted that we drifted off to sleep right away. In the wee hours of the morning the thundering sounds of machine guns woke us. We didn't panic anymore, although we still worried. We decided to remain in the same location. In the afternoon of the same day, Mouesse's water broke. My mother hurried to get the traditional midwife. I took a walk to the stream and waited there until Mouesse gave birth to a healthy and beautiful daughter. I returned to our location at sunset and found my mother holding the newborn, Mouesse looking exhausted, and Leolin smiling.

"Come and hold your niece, son," my mother smiled.

I was rooted in the same spot, as if I had just been hypnotized. The sight of a newborn made me remember and miss my whole childhood. I felt nostalgic. The only thing I cared about was playing daily and continuously. Life was so easy and everybody seemed happy. *How did we end up here?* I asked myself.

"Don't just stand there." She waved me over.

I suddenly snapped out of my daydreaming episode, hesitantly took two steps forward, extended my arms, and said, "Mum, I'm clumsy holding a newborn. I don't know how to do it."

"Don't worry, son. Come and I'll show you how to do it," she said.

The baby was neatly swaddled and under my mother's guidance and supervision, I took my niece into my arms with extra care and held her for a while. Our focus shifted from the enemies to the new addition to our family. She was quiet and looked very peaceful. I don't know if she could somehow sense we were in tremendous danger. She gave us no problems at all, which was a huge relief. A week after giving birth, Mouesse fell ill. She started to experience pain all over her body and couldn't breastfeed anymore. My mother and I learned how to make porridge with dried cassava roots mixed with sugar cane juice. We both took turns caring for the baby, which turned out to be a very good learning experience for me.

Days continued to pass with the enemies still running rampant. For a long time nothing seemed to change, however hard we prayed, believed, invoked, and implored God for a miracle. The more we prayed the worse the situation grew. While Mouesse was in recovery, we talked a lot about what she'd seen or heard during her stay in Bouansa.

"What was it like to have cold-blooded killers walk into your husband's tavern all the time?"

"To tell you the truth, it was definitely terrifying! But over time we got used to interacting with them."

"Yes, I can only imagine," I said.

"They were so arrogant and pompous! They would brag about the people they'd killed, their conquests, loots, and expensive lifestyles. That was quite an experience!"

"I suppose money, guns, and drugs got to their heads and they felt almighty and invincible."

"Unfortunately, that seemed to be the case for the majority of them, at least."

Mouesse paused for a few seconds, stared into the distance, tried to blink back her tears, which she wiped with her hand, and said, "I'm still utterly shocked by the level of their savagery! I remember one day they caught a woman with her two kids trying to walk across the Niari Bridge. They made the poor woman throw her kids into the river, one by one."

"In that crocodile-infested river?"

"Yes, in the Niari River. Held at gunpoint, the poor woman did as they ordered, and plunged into the river after her kids. To this day I still have nightmares about it."

"Wow! What a cruel country we live in!" I said.

I fell silent for a while and a lot of thoughts were going through mind. *Why can't humans live in peace and harmony? Why so much hate against one another?* I wondered. Mouesse was lying on the mattress and I was sitting alongside her on a tree trunk twiddling with my fingers.

"Poquito had joined the rebellion," I continued.

"Yes, I know. I was surprised and shocked to see him in a military uniform with the rebels in Bouansa."

"He was set up by his girlfriend and got killed in Mpanga."

"Oh my God! What happened?" she asked.

"Money was the reason for his murder."

"Really? It's hard to believe that Poquito is no longer with us."

"Yes, I know. He had four million CFA, which he looted when they conquered Nkayi, and his girlfriend lured him to move in with her in Mpanga. You know how Mpanga is full of bandits."

"Yes, I know! Mpanga has quite a reputation," she said.

"She had already conspired with the bandits to kill her boyfriend. They made the whole thing look like an armed robbery."

"I guess if you live by the sword you die by the sword."

"Yes indeed. One morning the bandits stormed into their house while Poquito and his girlfriend slept. They shot Poquito in cold blood and spared his girlfriend's life, according to the plan. The girlfriend and her partners in crime split the cash," I explained.

"I presume that is what you get when you associate with bitches and live a life of crime."

"He was such a shy and quiet kid growing up. I wonder where it all went wrong for him. He was such a talented soccer player!"

"Sad. People in Voungou will be shocked and heartbroken to hear Poquito's story! If he had stayed in Pointe-Noire with his father and brothers, he would still be alive today," Mouesse added.

We talked for hours about the rise and fall of the rebellion and reminisced about our childhood memories. Having Mouesse around made me feel better and a little more optimistic about our chances of survival. Somehow her mere presence always helped me picture myself back in Pointe-Noire, safe and sound.

KIMFINKOU

Weeks had elapsed with no sign of the enemies near Kimfinkou. Many villagers resolved to return to their homes. They surmised that there was no cause for concern anymore. Life slowly began to get back to normal. Other villagers timidly followed suit, as the enemies were still nowhere to be found in the area. But one morning, they paid Kimfinkou and the surrounding villages a surprise visit. They slew three high school teachers who were chatting and playing checkers on the side of the road. Many villagers managed to escape but they captured a few young men. The enemies dragged their prisoners back to their base camp. They tried interrogating them but got nowhere. So they asked them to say their last words, telling them:

"Say your last word
Before you exit this World!
In a few seconds, you shall die!
I have no mercy, however loud you cry!

I'm a killing machine
From a foreign country,
A cold-blooded mercenary.
I was paid to slay anyone!

I earnestly mean anyone
Who opposes the Lion's rise!
Today you shall serve as a lesson

To any foes that hinder the revolution.

This is the restoration of despotism;
The colonists approve of the system.
Why can't you surrender to this cause?
Close your eyes as you die in this blaze!

One of the prisoners nicknamed Gora pronounced his last words in Spanish, begging for mercy.

"¡No me maten, por favor! ¡Tengan piedad! !Suelténme, se lo suplico por favor!" he cried out with tears streaming down his face.

The enemies looked at each other in surprise; they paused, looked back at him and asked, "Você fala Português?"

"Nao posso falar Português mas eu entendo um poco," he replied.

"Você è um rebelde? Infiltrado?" they asked him.

"Não tenho nada que ver con la rebelión. Eu sou un estudiante de linguas estranjeras en la Universidad de Brazzaville," he replied

They untied Gora and decided to spare his life. They were so delighted to have finally found somebody in the middle of nowhere who could at least communicate with them. But they still held him captive, interrogating, talking, and trying to collect as much information as possible from him. Every morning the enemies continued spreading across the district to hunt. They always seemed to return to camp with captives. They would interrogate them and use Gora as a translator. They still decided which captives deserved to live and which ones deserved to die. Day by day Gora began to find more favor in the eyes of the enemies. They grew to like him and treated him as one of their own. He seized the opportunity to plead with the enemies to show compassion toward the poor population.

"The people of Mouyondzi didn't perpetrate the rebellion."

"Is that so?"

"Yes, it is. That's the truth. Thugs, crooks, and fools did. We're paying the price for a despicable movement that endangered our lives long before you came into Mouyondzi."

"Are you serious?"

"Yes, I'm serious. We denounced the rebellion from day one. If we the people of Mouyondzi had the power to dismantle it, we would have done that a long time ago. But these people were armed to the teeth. They could do whatever they wanted; that is why we find ourselves in this predicament today," Gora explained.

"Where are those thugs now? Could you identify them if you saw them?"

"The majority ran away. They're certainly outside Mouyondzi as we speak. They know what penalty awaits them if you ever catch them. Those hidden in the forests across Mouyondzi are innocent civilians who had no affiliation with the pathetic rebellion," Gora continued to educate them about the truth.

"Will there ever be anything for us to worry about if we sign peace agreements with your people?"

"There will be no irregularities from the people of Mouyondzi. We are a people of peace! You can trust me on this. I know my people," Gora said.

"We'll consult with our superiors first and tell you what we decide. Then we shall take it from there."

To be honest, I don't know whether the enemies were instructed by the government to make peace with us at that time, if they had grown tired of living here and wanted to go home, or if it was solely thanks to Gora's language skills. Needless to say, Gora played a crucial role in turning the situation around for the people. His presence in the enemies' camp helped them to gain firsthand information about the true side of the population. The miracle we all prayed and cried for over weeks was about to come to pass.

NKILA-POSTE TREATY

Rumors were circulating about a potential meeting on Saturday in Nkila-poste between chiefs of villages and heads of the government forces. The dry season was fast approaching. We wondered how to deal with the cold, drought, etc. On Saturday morning, we were chit-chatting when we heard people shouting, "Peace! Peace! Peace! You may all come out! Go back to your homes! The war is over!"

Everybody seemed uneasy, worried, scared, hesitant, and confused about the message.

"Did you hear, children? People are shouting peace! We're finally free!" my mother enthused.

"Don't get too excited, Mum. This could be a trap!" I warned.

"I don't think it is a trap this time. I'll walk around, talk to some people, and find out more."

My mother left at once. I didn't know what to make of it. However, I could sense change was on the horizon. Mouesse had almost made a full recovery and couldn't contain her excitement. She was holding her baby, her face gleaming with joy as she exclaimed, "This is wonderful news! How sweet the sound of freedom and peace!"

"We can't celebrate yet. The enemies could still conspire to annihilate us once we go back. You never know," I warned her.

"I'm sick and tired of running and hiding. Whatever happens to us happens. I'm fed up with this lifestyle. I want to go back home," she complained.

"Yes, I know, Mouesse. I'm just trying to be realistic. Let's wait and see what happens. Don't lose hope yet. This could well be the moment we've all be waiting for," I said.

The promise of peace sounded like the voice of an angel sent from Heaven to liberate us. I composed a piece of poetry to capture the emotions I was feeling inside at that moment.

For weeks in the wilderness
Outside walls of steel,
We were in prison, defenseless,
Persecuted by foreign thugs with zeal.

Each day was a struggle for survival.
Death, the slovenly thief, was on the prowl.
Human life was worthless.
Each day we lost peers and shed tears.

At the peak of our multiple woes,
We found mercy in the eyes of our foes.
The agreements of peace have been signed;
No more shall they hunt us down, our foes vowed.

Home sweet home! Let's go, we can cope!
The persecution is over altogether.
Let us return to our homes together,
For today is a brand new day, full of hope!

While my mother was out and about, Houdini showed up at our hiding spot. He had no difficulty finding us wherever the location. Thank goodness he was not the hunter we all dreaded!

"There he comes again, the uninvited and unwanted guest!" I whispered to Mouesse as I saw him approach.

"How is everybody today? Mouesse, your baby is so cute!" Houdini started.

"Thanks Houdini," Mouesse said.

"The war is over! We've done it. We negotiated and signed the peace agreement with the government. There is nothing to fear anymore! We can all go back to our homes! That is the good news I came to share with you!" he said with a big smile on his face.

After Houdini had left our camp, our mother returned.

"It's over! We can go back home now!" she said excitedly.

"Are you absolutely sure about this?" I asked.

"Yes! I spoke with a few people who confirmed the information. There is nothing to be afraid of anymore," she explained.

I guess I had to trust my mother and everybody else. We packed up our belongings and walked back to Nkenge along with everybody else. Everywhere I looked there were groups of relieved-looking people talking and trekking back home. My mother's home resembled an ill-kept animal sanctuary. There were spiders, rats, cockroaches, frogs, and snakes. We got rid of them, cleaned up the place, and moved back in. Lots of huts still missed doors, windows, and roofs. Villagers helped one another rebuild, repair, and readjust to normal life.

THE WAY FORWARD

On Sunday, I couldn't wait to go to Nkila-poste. I was eager to exit Mouyondzi as quickly as possible and desperately wished I could take my whole family with me. I became paranoid and my out-of-control mind started inventing scenarios where the whole district relapsed into organized chaos again. So I talked to my mother about my plan.

"Mum, I want to go Nkila-poste today," I started.

"Forget it! It is way too soon to go there!"

"Mum, I want to get the hell out of here as soon as possible," I insisted.

"Yes, I know. Let's wait a week at least. Although we're supposedly free now, there will still be irregularities here and there," she said.

"Not a week, please, Mum! I can't wait a week," I pleaded.

"You don't have a choice! This is not up for discussion! You have to wait! When the time is right, I shall go with you to Nkila-poste. Understood?" she barked.

I was very well familiar with that tone of voice. When we were kids, it served as a warning; if or when we ignored it, a proper beating would ensue. Although times had changed and I was older now, I knew not to cross my mother. I felt very frustrated but kept everything bottled up inside. I used that time to visit family and helped out wherever I was needed. I would hang out with Noko Mwini and my cousins.

Noko Moussoki's condition was yet to improve. His face was bandaged; he had lost a lot of weight, looked frail, and had to be fed. People in the village were very supportive and helpful. Everybody tried to help him as best they could.

Every day the government forces would visit villages, intermingle, and interact with the people, behaving like Red Cross volunteers on a humanitarian mission. The rebels got rid of their guns and would vanish into thin air every time the government forces were in the vicinity. Over time, they realized that they were no longer in danger, so they stopped running and gradually reintegrated into the community. The reconciliation was real and the new administration was open to collaborate and work with everybody.

Houdini resumed his normal life and went back to farming. The government forces began to endear themselves to some guys and local girls. Friendship and romance blossomed here and there. Business resumed. The weekend market was reopened. Life was quickly getting back to normal. The government sent helicopters to help stranded civil servants return to work. Noko Moussoki, accompanied by his mother, wouldn't pass up the opportunity. They made the trip to Nkila-poste on foot and somehow got there. His mother helped plead his case with the officials.

"This is my son Moussoki, who got shot," she explained.

"Why did he get shot? Was he part of the rebellion?" they asked.

"Moussoki works for CFCEO. He had nothing to do with the rebellion," she clarified.

"If you claim your son is a CFCEO employee, what was he doing here in the first place? Why wasn't he in Brazzaville or Pointe-Noire working?"

"So-so-r-ry, I-I-I," he stuttered, trying to convey his message with hand gestures.

"You're no CFCEO employee! You're an infiltrado! A former rebel!" they interjected.

"He is my son. He was not affiliated with the rebellion. He didn't have anything to do with it. Please, help us, help him!" my grandmother begged.

"Sorry, grandma! Our government can't help traitors! There is absolutely nothing we can do for him!" they said, waving them away.

Noko Moussoki and his mother were deflated; they couldn't believe that the officials mandated to assist the population had turned them away. To add salt to injury, they had to make the long trip back home on foot. Times got harder as he was made to wait a while longer. The railroad was still paralyzed. In a country where people destroy faster than they rebuild, we all feared he was likely going to rot alive in the forsaken land of his ancestors. In desperation my grandmother showed up at my mother's house. She looked worried, sad, and defeated.

"I don't know who else to turn to for help," she stated.

"Mum, I heard the government is helping civil servants in Nkila-poste," my mother said.

"We went there today but they wouldn't help. They even accused Moussoki of being a former rebel before dismissing us."

"I'm sorry to hear it, Mum. I guess we all have to wait until the roads are restored. CFCEO will certainly help him get back," my mother said.

My grandmother nodded her disapproval, scratched her head, looked at my mother, and bluntly asked, "Could you please lend your brother some money to make the trip to Brazzaville?"

"Mum, where would I get money from?" she pouted with disgust.

"Didn't my grandson come here to sell some fabrics?" she inquired.

"So? What do you expect him to do?" my mother asked in a frustrated tone of voice.

"Please lend us some money! I'll pay you back. You can't stand by and watch your brother rot alive here, can you?" my grandmother pleaded.

"Mum, you like making me angry, don't you? Huh?" she asked, sounding confrontational.

"Forgive me, child. I'm desperate and don't know who else to turn to," my grandmother sheepishly replied.

"Why would you assume the fabrics sold? Even if the fabrics sold, the money is still my ex-husband's, not my son's. Neither my son nor I have any money to loan you!" she stormed and walked away.

I felt for my grandmother but I also counted on that money, which wasn't a certainty, to be honest. A week had passed and as it concluded, my mother and I went to Nkila-poste.

"Go ahead, son. I have some friends to catch up with at the market," she said.

"Okay! Where shall I meet you, Mum?" I asked.

"Let's meet back here in about half an hour," she replied.

I walked straight to Papa Ndazet's. I was relieved to see they were all alive and well. Papa Ndazet was sitting on a wooden bench by the door, looking pensive. He rose to his feet when he saw me and gave me a hug.

"Welcome back, son! Thank goodness we all survived!" he sighed.

"It's been a very tough time!" I said.

"Yes, it has been tough. My grocery store was pillaged and I lost all my merchandise," he said as he motioned me to follow him inside the house.

"I'm sorry, Papa Ndazet."

"It's okay. What matters is that we all made it unscathed. Wait here. I'm going to get your money," he said.

My heart skipped a beat upon hearing his last words. I sat at the table and waited while he quickly went inside his bedroom. He came back holding a black purse. He unzipped it and said, "Here is your money."

I couldn't believe my eyes and was lost for words. *What a pleasant surprise!* I thought.

"Thank you very much, Papa Ndazet!" I smiled.

"You're welcome, son! You have a safe trip back home and may the ancestors be with you!"

I removed my shoes, hid the money in my socks, and put my shoes back on. I hugged and waved goodbye to everybody and rejoined my mother, who was patiently waiting for me.

"How did it go?" she asked.

"He gave me my money in full!" I enthused.

"I'm not surprised. Ndazet is the most reliable, trustworthy, and dependable person I know," she confided.

We did a bit of grocery shopping and walked back, discussing the travel options available to me.

"You can't fly directly from here to Pointe-Noire unless you're willing to wait a few more weeks," my mother said.

"No way, Mum! I can't wait any longer. I just can't," I replied, nodding my opposition.

"Okay. The only option left is to walk to Nkayi and catch a direct flight from there to Pointe-Noire," she explained.

"That sounds more like it. I like that option," I smiled.

"We now have to find some people who are walking to Nkayi so that you can tag along," she said.

Every now and then we would come across the government forces walking up and down the streets or driving slowly from village to village, interacting with the villagers. We avoided eye contact with them. Despite the official peace agreements in place, these were still trained killers. They still had the authority to take anyone's life. All in all, everything went smoothly.

My return to Pointe-Noire was beginning to look more and more like a certainty. My mother made some enquiries around. Some friends of hers were returning to Nkayi and they offered to take me with them. I was excited and a little sad at the same time. Everything was surreal. My mother was experiencing mixed emotions, which in my creative mind sounded more like this:

"Dear son, run for your life;
As fast as you can, escape!
I'll try to survive this strife.
Go and hide away in the Western Cape!

Don't worry about me, angel!
I shall be okay in these gory places.
I don't want to see you blaze in hell,
In a hell of bullets burning innocent faces.

I hate to see you leave
But am glad you're rushing someplace quiet.
Send me a postcard on Christmas Eve,
So I can rejoice in this war-torn site."

Saying goodbye to loved ones has always been emotionally hard, especially when you don't know whether you're going to see them again or not. I went to say goodbye to Noko Mwini.

"We made it, nephew! What an experience that was!" he sighed.

"Yes indeed! I don't even know where start!" I echoed his thoughts.

"Have a safe trip back and may the ancestors be with you!"

He hugged me goodbye; I went to my grandmother's and quickly said goodbye to everybody. Noko Moussoki's condition was stable but he still needed medical attention. He was lying in bed, staring at the ceiling. He didn't turn to look at me or say anything to me. He was in constant pain. I felt a bit guilty we couldn't loan my grandmother the money. There was just not enough money to cover the travel expenses for two people.

Back at my mother's, I had all my things neatly packed inside my duffle bag. I held my niece for a while and talked to Mouesse, whose husband was scheduled to come and pick her up later that day. I hugged Leolin and my mother accompanied me to the meeting point. Minutes later her friends showed up. I hugged my mother, and there were tears from both sides. She bid me goodbye and promised to come and see us in Pointe-Noire in a month or so.

There were nine of us in the group. We left on September 6,

My itinerary To Pointe - Noire

September 6th, 1999

8:00 am From NKenge — Kibounda

September 7th, 1999

6:00 am From Kibounda — Kimboukou
9:13 am From Kimboukou — Kiyangala

September 8th, 1999

5:50 am From Kiyangala — MBamba 9:00 am
10:00 am From MBamba — MBISI-MPATI 10:53 am

September 9th 1999

5 am From MBISI-MPATI — SEKE-PEMBE 7:55 am
8:55 am From SEKE PEMBE — Marquis 9:10 am
9:10 am From Marquis — Kimeni 10:45 am
11:00 am From Kimeni — MBouma 12:00 Pm
12:00 Pm From MBouma — MBEMBE-MBOTE 5:00 Pm
6 Pm From MBEMBE-MBOTE — NKAYI 8:00 Pm

My itinerary

121

1999, at precisely 8am. Everywhere I looked, there were people walking in all directions. We trekked for six hours through forests, trudged up the hills and across shallow streams, until we arrived at a big river that led to a small village called Kibounda. We stood on the riverbank along with other travelers, waiting for the canoe to take us across. There was only one wooden canoe available and it could only transport six passengers at a time. I was scared when I noticed the back of the canoe slightly sank in the water under our weight. My mind went out of control and started replaying all the dreadful stories I had heard about drowning or crocodiles killing people. But the determination to get back home gave me nerves of steel. So I focused and kept my composure. I remained motionless as the skipper expertly paddled the canoe safely toward dry land.

We finally made it to Kibounda as the sun was disappearing behind a veil of dark clouds. The people of that village were very hospitable and welcomed us with open arms. The village chief led us to a shelter they had reserved for refugees. We all rested and spent the night there. There were no telephones, Internet, or Wi-Fi so I could not communicate with my mother to keep her updated on the progress of my journey back to Pointe-Noire. In the days that followed, we covered long distances through forests, across streams and rivers, past villages, and up mountains and hills. Four days later, we finally made it to Nkayi, safe and sound. My walking companions helped me find the address I was looking for. I arrived at my mother's friend's house and she welcomed me with open arms.

"Welcome to Nkayi, son! You made it safe and sound," Ma Louzolo smiled.

"Thank you," I sheepishly said.

"How was the walk?" she asked.

"It was very long and difficult but overall okay," I explained.

"You must be starving and exhausted. Let me show you to your room," she said as she led me to the guest room, which reminded me of my own room back home. Four days of walking across unfamiliar territories had worn me out. I had blisters on the soles of my feet, as well as my hands and shoulders. I got myself cleaned and Ma Louzolo knocked on my door.

"I made you some dinner. Come and eat before you go to bed," she said.

I joined Ma Louzolo and her family at the table. I ate my dinner fast and in silence, only smiling each time my eyes met theirs. I finished my dinner, said thank you and goodnight to Ma Louzolo and her family, and called it a day.

I had no intention of staying in Nkayi for more than two days. There were soldiers everywhere and I felt uneasy and very nervous. Like every civilian there, I needed police clearance before I could freely walk the streets. I felt like an immigrant in my own country. The police were running a background check on everybody entering the city. They had a blacklist with names of individuals they wanted to arrest and slay. Ma Louzolo accompanied me to the nearest police station. I filled out a form, answered their routine why, who, what, when, where, and how questions, and the police officer said, "Come back here tomorrow morning."

Under normal circumstances, I wouldn't have any cause for concern. But in those days, one never knew. I was concerned about the unknown criteria by which they determined eligibility for police clearance. I heard stories about innocent people whose names were mistakenly blacklisted, and the rest you can easily imagine. My freedom depended solely upon the issuance of that document. I kept counting the hours, hoping and praying that everything would go according to plan. I still couldn't believe I'd made it this far. The word relieved couldn't even begin to describe how I felt. The two days there went by so quickly, and I was granted police clearance. I thanked my very generous and kind hostess for her hospitality and for helping me throughout the whole process. I caught a taxi that took me directly to the airport.

EN ROUTE TO POINTE-NOIRE

While waiting for my turn to buy a ticket, I was surprised to bump into a former classmate from high school named Elombe. I couldn't believe my eyes when I saw him in a military uniform. In high school, he was such a bright young man who did well in his studies. I thought he would grow up to become a well-respected politician or university professor. To my surprise, he instead opted to join the army right after high school. He was then deployed in Nkayi as part of the intervention units tasked with restoring law and order in the south of the country.

"Hey, Lazare! What are you doing in this part of the country? I thought you were studying in Brazzaville," Elombe said as he gave me a massive brotherly hug.

"I went to visit my family in Mouyondzi and got stuck there," I confided.

Although he was my former classmate, I was not prepared to pour out my heart about the ordeal that I had just gone through. I kept the conversation short. All I wanted was to get out of there as quickly as possible so that I could see my family again. I sensed that he tacitly understood me.

"I really am sorry to hear that, my brother. But thank goodness you're alive! Let me help you get your ticket. Come with me."

Elombe and I pushed our way past a group of people and soldiers standing around, eating, drinking, or smoking. They looked rather confused, but I did not care since I had one of them protecting me. I couldn't care less about what they were thinking. Nkayi's airport did not look like an airport at all. I

NOMS _Kokolo_

PRENOMS _Lazare_

DATE ET LIEU DE N_____

NATIONALITE _Congolaise_

FILS (FILLE) DE: _Kokolo Lazare_

ET DE: _Noussounga - Kinbolo_

ADRESSE: _____

NOMS ET PRENOMS DE (DE LA) CONJOINT(E)

_____

PROFESSION: _Eleve_

PASSEPORT OU CARTE D'_____

DATE ET LIEU DE DELIVRANCE: _____

FAIT A PONT, LE _11/02/99_

LE CHEF DE SERVICE DE POLICE AREI
LANCE.

L'INTERESSE(E)

Sergent
Maurice-EBOU

My Police Clearance

don't remember seeing a control tower anywhere. If there was no airplane there, one could easily mistake it for a desolate large rice field. There was a runway and four coffee tables alongside it. These coffee tables served as counters where passengers purchased tickets. Additionally, there was a small kiosk next to the coffee tables, which men in military uniforms used as a tax office. Since I was with Elombe, I was able to purchase my one-way ticket to Pointe-Noire without spending a single cent on those fabricated taxes.

"Take care of yourself, Lazare," Elombe said as we hugged each other goodbye.

I got on the plane bound for Pointe-Noire. It was the very first time that I had flown. I felt both nervous and excited at the same time and I felt like a VIP as I occupied my very comfortable seat and buckled my seat belt. After enduring almost a year of constant persecution, I felt like I was going through a resurrection. The sight of two soldiers on board brought back the memory of my eventful train ride to Mouyondzi. Fortunately, they were not allowed to carry their weapons on the plane. As soon as they boarded the plane, they obediently gave their weapons to the flight attendant, who in turn stored them away. I heaved a sigh of relief because I knew I wouldn't suffer the same abuse as I did on the train ride a year ago.

It was about 9am when the airplane departed from Nkayi. For the first time in a long time I felt free and a little relaxed. I felt like a normal law-abiding citizen with rights. I heaved a sigh of relief as we ascended toward the sky! The airplane sped across the sky, and Nkayi looked like a speck of dust that gradually disappeared before my eyes. We landed at 11am at the Pointe-Noire international airport. I was very delighted and felt so relieved to be back in my comfort zone again, my city. I felt as if everything was welcoming me back home. I got off the airplane, strode toward the taxi rank, caught the first taxi I saw, and headed straight home to Voungou. "Home sweet home, indeed!" I exclaimed out loud.

HOME SAFE AND SOUND

When I returned to Voungou, neighbors, friends, and family all crowded at our house to see me. Everybody was both happy to see me again and very interested in hearing about my experience.

I looked sick, malnourished, and brittle. It felt and looked as if I had just risen from the dead. Everybody who knew me was showing me so much unconditional love and empathy. I felt great and words could not express the flood of emotions I was feeling inside. I was experiencing the fullness of joy. I felt very fortunate to be reunited with my family, friends, and loved ones. To be honest, after almost a year hiding and running in the jungles from the rebels and the army, I had grown very pessimistic about my chances of survival. So many people were brutally killed every day that I kept wondering whether I would make it out of there alive or not. Being back in Pointe-Noire, alive and well, felt more like a dream than reality. I had to pinch myself a few times to make sure I was not dreaming. I took a shower, had the biggest meal my stomach could handle, and slowly drifted off to sleep. When I woke up, I felt rested, grabbed a pen, a piece of paper, and wrote three letters, one addressed to my mother to inform her that I had arrived safely, one to Noko Mwini to thank him for everything, and the last one to Papa Ndazet to express my heartfelt gratitude to him for being who he was. I placed the letters in A4 khaki envelopes and set them on my bedside table. In the evening we all sat around the table.

"Dad, you see—we nearly lost Lazare! He is very lucky to have survived. So many people died during the bloody rebellion."

"I know and I'm truly sorry, Judith," he apologized.

"I hope you won't make the same mistake twice, Dad."

"Calm down, Judith. You should let it go. We should be celebrating that I made it," I interrupted.

"What about university? You missed the whole year," Judith reminded me.

"I'm not sending him to Brazzaville. The Ninjas have been launching sporadic attacks on the city," my father said. "Do you remember Willmart's brother, Devon?"

"Yes, what about him?" I inquired.

"He was killed during one of those sporadic attacks," Judith informed me.

"That's horrible!"

"Remember Ntakom, my cousin? He lived with us in Mpaka. You were still a year old at the time," my father said.

"Yes, ya Ntakom?" I asked.

"The very same. He also got killed in Brazzaville."

"But why? Wasn't he an army officer?" I asked.

"Yes, he was," my father replied, sounding sad.

"What did he do? What happened?"

I could tell my father was still hurting; he looked up, fighting back the tears for a second, looked back at me and said, "After the war in Brazzaville, the new government mandated all civil servants to return to work. Ntakom went back and got shot by the army two days later."

"Wow...how shocking! But I still don't understand why they killed him," I said.

"We don't really know all the details. Maybe he had a conflict with the army, or maybe because he was from the south...to tell you the truth, I don't know."

The room went quiet for a while. I couldn't believe how many innocent lives fell victim to a senseless civil war and rebellion.

"The political situation has been slowly getting back to normal nationwide. But I won't risk sending you to Brazzaville.

I'm going to sell the rental property that's there and send you overseas instead," he said.

"That's an excellent idea, Dad!" Judith enthused.

I looked at my father and didn't say anything, but my smile said it all. I was looking forward to it.

"When I return from my trip, we'll explore our options and take it from there," he said.

My younger sisters were just smiling, playing around, and enjoying themselves while the adults were in serious conversation. My father soon sent them to bed, started yawning himself and called it a night. Judith and I continued talking.

"Your friends kept coming here asking for you. Ntsayi particularly asked for you a lot," she said.

"Aww. I love Ntsayi. You have no idea how much I missed all my friends," I said.

"Yes, I can only imagine."

"I'll go and see him tomorrow."

"His father got him a job at the Harbor."

"Oh! Lucky him! Do you know what kind of job it is?"

"You can ask when you see him next time. I don't know all the details."

I was soon starting to yawn myself, and the cuckoo clock on the wall read 11:50pm. I wished Judith goodnight and went to bed. I had nightmares in my sleep, woke up a couple of times, restless, and tossed and turned. I lay flat, eyes wide open, and stared at the ceiling, my mind replaying the experiences I had gone through, and my brain was frazzled. I don't remember falling back asleep. All I remember was getting up to the neighbors' roosters' cock-a-doodle-dooing. I felt a little disoriented for a second in my own room.

I grabbed a towel, wrapped it around my waist, picked up a steel bucket by our avocado tree, walked to our well, and waited for my turn. Our tenant's wife was busy filling up her 25 liter yellow plastic drum and two buckets with water. We had a quick conversation. I got my water and took a shower.

The sunrise was wonderful as always, and the familiar noise, the hustle and bustle of Voungou made me smile. I felt as if somebody was constantly tickling me. I joined my family at the table; we ate breakfast, talked, joked, played around, and dispersed. An hour later, Ntsayi dropped by and gave me a big and warm hug.

"Welcome back, Frangin! I was very worried! I'm very delighted that you made it!" he exclaimed.

"Thank you, Ntsayi! Me too!" I said as we sat by the avocado tree in the corner of our property.

"Judith told me you're now working in the harbor."

"Yes, I am, for the time being."

"What about your trip to Paris?"

"I had complications at the embassy for the visa. My application was declined twice already."

"Oh! I'm really sorry to hear that."

"Thanks. It's okay. I'm no longer upset about it. My side businesses are still doing well, and I'm now working."

"Wow! That's brilliant, Ntsayi! Good for you, Frangin! What do you do at your job?"

"I operate forklifts, check delivery, and register the workers' hours at the end of the day."

I congratulated him and also told him about my father's plan to send me overseas. We were happy for each other, talked some more, and said goodbye. I retrieved the letters from the bookshelf in my room, folded them, and put them in my pants' side pocket. I walked to the corner of Avenue de la Liberté, caught a taxi and went to OCH for a visit. My cousins weren't home, and Noko Loussoukou was patting his way around the living room, trying to sweep the floor.

I walked in and announced myself. "Noko Loussoukou! How are you doing today?"

"Oh! Lazare? Is that you?" he asked.

"Yes, it's me, Noko Loussoukou," I replied.

He patted his way around the table, slowly walked toward the back of the leather sofa, carefully edged round it and sat down.

"Thank God you made it! I was very worried about you. I confronted your father about it. For goodness sake! Why did he send you there?" He shook his head in disbelief. He paused for a few seconds and said, "Your father is a successful entrepreneur, but sometimes the things he does leave a lot to be desired."

Here we go again with the blame game, I thought. I was sitting on the couch in front of him. I didn't how to respond, so I kept quiet.

"Are you okay? I was informed Dad passed away and the government forces shot Moussoki. How is he holding up? How is my mum coping?"

"Sadly, yes. Grandpa passed away after a short illness. Nobody knew what the cause of the illness was. He refused to be taken to a hospital," I explained.

"That's very sad indeed," he said, scratching his head.

"Noko Moussoki got shot by the Angolan soldiers in Mouandi on his way from Mouzanga. Kihoulou and the kids went to stay with her parents. So Noko Moussoki couldn't stand not seeing his family."

"Why would Kihoulou make such a drastic move? Were they having marital problems?"

"Not that I was aware of. She didn't feel safe in Nkenge. She desperately wanted to be with her folks."

"How is my mum coping?"

"Grandma is managing and she gets a lot of help from the family and neighbors. Everybody has been very supportive and helpful."

"Very good!" he sighed.

There was a moment of silence; Noko Loussoukou had his eyes focused on where he believed I was sitting, trying to connect all the dots in his head, and said, "I contacted my superiors at the Chemin de fer, and they have arranged for Moussoki's transfer to a hospital in France. They'll be sending agents there to help him and facilitate the transfer in about two weeks."

"That's wonderful news, Noko Loussoukou! What a relief!" I sighed.

There was silence again, and then Noko Loussoukou said, "Kindoumba was incarcerated in Brazzaville for months."

"What? Noko Kindoumba? What did he do?"

"Yes, your uncle. He served in Pascal Lissouba's administration. As you already know, he was in the air force, worked both as a mechanic and pilot. He was accused of fighting for Pascal Lissouba during the civil war," he explained.

"That's absurd! What happened to him after that?"

"It was worrying and depressing for all us!" he said.

"I can imagine," I said.

"He was taken to a court martial, where he was found not guilty of all charges. He was released not long ago. Things in this country have definitely got worse."

"Yes, it's depressing, to say the least."

"Yes indeed. Currently, in the Pool region, innocent civilians are caught in a war between government forces and rebels."

I was getting tired of talking about the killing and war, so I tried to change the subject. "I'm trying to get some letters to Noko Mwini, Papa Ndazet, and Mum. Do you have any connections to help me?"

"Yes. Leave them with me, and I'll have my connections get them there."

I pulled the letters out of my pocket, and he told me where to leave them. We talked for hours, my cousins finally came home, and I caught up with all of them. I left OCH and decided to walk back to Voungou. I wanted to enjoy my new lease on life, breathe in the fresh air, and experience the sense of normalcy again.

ASYLUM OVERSEAS

The tough experiences I had to endure in Mouyondzi forced my life to take a detour and influenced the course of my destiny. They set in motion a sequence of events that impacted my personality, changed my perspective on life, and directed my steps to where I am today. I learned to appreciate life and people more, to make every second of my existence count, not to take anything or anybody for granted. I understood that tomorrow was never guaranteed, and I also understood the meaning of the saying, "Live each day as if it was your last."

After I had survived both the rebellion and the government armed forces' invasion of my parents' villages, I no longer saw a future for young people like myself in Congo. There was still an atmosphere of insecurity looming over the nation. My beloved country was no longer safe, and young people from the south of Congo in particular were enduring so much persecution. Brazzaville was still suffering sporadic armed attacks by the rebels (Ninjas) from the Pool region in the south of Congo. These rebels were comprised of militants loyal to the main opposition leader, Bernard Kolelas, who had been forced out of the country. During one of those sporadic attacks, Marien Ngouabi University was invaded. Ninjas engaged the government armed forces in battle, students got caught in the middle, and many perished.

It seemed that joining the newly assembled Congolese army was both a safe haven and an escape route for a hopeless, despondent, and defeated generation. Needless to say, I did not once contemplate the idea of joining the army. My main objective still was to study law at university. Unfortunately, University Marien Ngouabi in Brazzaville was no longer an option. I felt very frustrated because I couldn't pursue my dream. The detailed plan I had devised to study law and eventually become a judge was beginning to fall apart. My father saw and understood my frustration. He then decided to sell one of his properties that was vandalized in Brazzaville. He made enough money from the sale to finance my trip to South Africa to seek asylum.

As a refugee in a foreign country, I faced other challenges and my priorities changed accordingly. I had to work extra hard to make ends meet. For the first time in my life, I had to look after myself financially. I had more responsibilities and bills to pay. My family also expected me to send them money every now and then. I could not afford university studies. I had so much happening at the same time that I did not think of applying for a scholarship. My father no longer sent me money because he was convinced that South Africa offered enough opportunities for me to be able to look after myself, which was true to a certain degree.

I settled for short and affordable courses that would help me become employable in the South African job market. In Cape Town, I obtained certificates in hotel reception, TEFL, and oral competency in Italian. My dream to study law and become a judge faded away over time. I started saving as much money as I could to invest into real estate back home.

As years went by, I developed a keen interest in observing human behavior. A new dream was born in my heart. I wanted to study psychology to help people as best I could. It wasn't until later, when I moved to the US, that I had the opportunity to study and complete my Bachelor's degree in Psychology.

LESSONS LEARNED AND REFLECTIONS

When I look back on everything that transpired in Mouyondzi, I come to the conclusion that life is too short and full of pleasant and unpleasant surprises. In the blink of an eye, one's life could end abruptly or change radically and dramatically. I had some important life choices to make to define the type of person I was to become for the rest of my days. The suffering that I witnessed and endured inspired me to grow into a better social being. We're all foreigners on this planet; our stay on Earth is temporary and fleeting. One day we're here, alive and well; the next we're gone forever. Why must we have so much hatred and animosity unto one another? What joy is there in inflicting pain or any form of suffering upon one another? Why do some humans revel in destroying the lives of others? These were and are to this day some of the questions to which I keep struggling to find answers. But instead of seeking answers in others, I realized that change for a better world begins with me. I choose to practice unconditional love toward fellow humans. I believe in unconditional love as a powerful force capable of ending all the senseless wars and making this world a better place.

www.ingramcontent.com/pod-product-compliance
Lightning Source LLC
Chambersburg PA
CBHW070808280326
41934CB00012B/3102